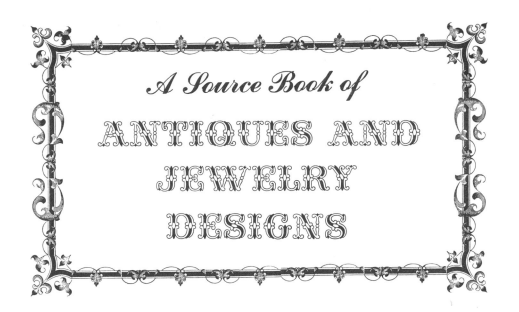

A Source Book of

ANTIQUES AND JEWELRY DESIGNS

A Source Book of

ANTIQUES AND JEWELRY DESIGNS

*Containing over 3800 Engravings
of Victorian Americana
including Jewelry, Silverware, Clocks,
Cutlery, Glassware, Musical Instruments,
etc., etc., etc.*

BY

CLARENCE P. HORNUNG

A DA CAPO PAPERBACK

Library of Congress Cataloging in Publication Data

Hornung, Clarence Pearson, comp.
  A source book of antiques and jewelry designs.

  (Da Capo Press paperback)
  Reprint of the ed. published by G. Braziller,
New York.
    1. Americana — Catalogs. 2. Antiques — United
States — Catalogs. 3. Art industries and trade,
Victorian — United States — Catalogs. I. Title.
II. Title: Antiques and jewelry designs.
  [NK807.H6 1977]   745.1'0973   77-10003
  ISBN 0-306-80070-5

ISBN: 0-306-80070-5

First Paperback Edition 1977

This Da Capo Press paperback edition of *A Source
Book of Antiques and Jewelry Designs* is an unabridged
republication of the first edition published in
New York in 1968. It is reprinted by arrangement
with George Braziller.

Published by Da Capo Press, Inc.
A Subsidiary of Plenum Publishing Corporation
227 West 17th Street
New York, New York 10011

PREFACE

1895 ... U.S.A. Just a few years before, at the great Chicago exposition celebrating the four hundred years since Columbus' discovery of the New World, millions were treated to unforgettable sights and scenes showing this country's impressive industrial growth. On the one hand, a burgeoning prosperity was reaching out to touch more and more of the people. On the other, a severe depression had thrown large numbers out of work and prices and wages plunged downward as Coxey's army descended on Washington to demand redress and fair employment.

But in spite of social unrest, labor riots and falling wages the general economic trend was upward. Giant strides were registered on a broad front. The railroads were adding thousands of miles of feeder lines to their major trunks, forging a network that reached into the tiniest hamlets for the delivery of goods and the exchange of farm produce. Cyclists in increasing numbers took to the rutted roads in a nationwide craze that resulted in better highways, just in time to pave the way for the slowly emerging horseless carriages of Olds, Ford, Haynes and Duryea. Farms grew larger and more productive as newer agricultural machinery, improved mowers, reapers and combines meant bumper crops and more money in the farmer's pocket. Everywhere, factory wheels turned faster. A larger proportion of Americans were preoccupied with the concern of business and the complicated operations of the new industrial economy.

It was into such a milieu of expanding activity that the demand for better merchandise and luxury goods was particularly marked. The plain household wares of an earlier era, expressing the strictly utilitarian needs of a simpler day and age, no longer satisfied Americans of the Nineties. They had been introduced to sophisticated continental styling at both the Centennial and Columbian exhibitions. The many popular women's journals brought the latest fashion notes to the most isolated towns. The mail-order catalogs arriving at regular intervals whetted milady's appetite regardless of whether she dwelled in the hinterlands or on Back Street in the Big City. No single force exerted a greater pulling power than the pages of these "wishing books," as the illustrated catalogs were called, designed to cater to "the wants of the Patrons of Husbandry." Where else could Ma Perkins of Sauk Center shop for goods and enjoy such delightful *divertissement* as in the thousand-paged tomes of Sears or Montgomery Ward? Where else could she find such a mad bazaar of tempting bargains but in the crowded showcase of these catalog pages?

We must remember that during the decade before the turn of the century the greater numbers of Americans still worked the farms or followed pursuits dictated by an agrarian economy. The masses had not yet been lured away by the attractions of our metropolitan centers. The sprawling country store or the corner jewelry shop at Main and Jefferson could not possibly carry a full line of merchandise in all areas. And so the astute proprietor supplemented his lavish displays with the big, fat, colorful catalogs supplied by the larger New York and Chicago mercantile houses without sizeably increasing his inventory.

The jewelry sections of these inviting volumes presented a confusing array of watches, chatelaines, pins, rings, brooches and fraternal ornaments in endless variety. Nowhere was the customer offered a more confusing choice than in the large selection of ladies and gents watches, their crystal covers of base or precious metal adorned in the riotous designs of contemporary inspiration. Amid the variety of watchcases that flowered in heterogenous profusion, certain

motifs were dominant, among them: 1) The Noble Stag, either at bay with lowered and threatened antlers or standing in all his forest-primeval majesty. 2) The Little Birds, swooning amid honeysuckle or carrying streamers of ribbon in their gold-filled beaks to the little gray home in the West. 3) The Iron Horse, generally depicted coming down the mountain, a black belching avalanche sweeping everything before it, or gliding on high-driving wheels over the wooden railroad trestle. Such was the skill and ingenuity of American watchcase artists in their avoidance of monotonous treatment that they easily outrivaled jewelry craftsmen of all preceding ages. While their motifs may have been limited in number, their capriciousness seemed to flow from an inexhaustible well. When not concentrating on the popularly-accepted themes, their ornamental variations, the full use of foliated scrolls and rococo beading, produced dazzling cases enhanced by engine-turning on exposed areas of plain metal.

When a man bought a timepiece it was inevitable that he also acquired a fob to properly chain it down across waistcoat and waistline. One would think such a watch chain offered only sterile possibilities to the gold-filledsmith, but here, again, the anonymous artists of that day came through with bright notions in link designs, variable combinations and permutations to have filled dozens of catalog pages with hundreds of exciting offerings.

From many of these chains were suspended the attached emblems of the Masons, the Elks, the Woodmen of the World, the Knights of Pythias, the Moose, the Redmen, the Brotherhood of Railroad Engineers, the Wheelmen of America, and other insignia of that vast fraternity of lodge members numbering in the millions. Gilbert K. Chesterton, writing in *What I Saw in America* about a man he met while traveling in Oklahoma, commented that he saw "a lean, brown man having the look of a shabby tropical traveler, with a grey moustache and a lively and alert eye. But the most singular thing about him was that the front of his coat was covered with a multitude of shining metallic emblems made in the shape of stars and crescents. I was well accustomed by this time to Americans adorning the lapels of their coats with little symbols of various societies; it is a part of the American passion for the ritual of comradeship. There is nothing that an American likes so much as to have a secret society, and make no secret of it."

The chatelaine watch was worn attached to the shirtwaist, the coat or any outer garment, and because it was highly conspicuous, designers sought to make it beautiful in a ladylike way. Some models had fleur-de-lis inlays on gold or were decorated with handsomely engraved flowers whose delicate convolutions covered the entire case.

Europeans have always been puzzled with our primary preoccupation with time. Farmer or factory worker, housewife or house painter, the ubiquitous timepiece had always been in evidence, whether dangling from a fob, pinned to a coat or worn on the wrist as if to advertise one had time on his hands. But the mantel clock of the Nineties, if not a thing of beauty by our modern standards, was a symbol of the décor of the decade. A clock can be ornamental as well as useful, and for centuries the world's clockmakers, as though fascinated by the mysterious time-substance marking beginning, transition and end, have exhausted their ingenuity on instruments beautiful to the eye which record the immortal march of the stars. Clocks came in wood, metal and marbleized imitation onyx case which closely resembles Mexican onyx so that it cannot be detected except by an expert. Elaborately incised with scrolls or frets, or appliqued with pseudo-ormolu mountings, the surface of these marbleized mantelpieces was anything but restful in appearance. Surmounted by figures of Boadicea or Victoria, broad-hatted cavaliers or Venetian gondoliers, there was a broad choice of sculptural designs to please every taste. A most popular type was personified by the pensive figure of a sandalshod goddess, one hand resting on a lyre at her side and the other supporting an evidently aching head. The carved or pressed wooden wall clocks, whose main function was to strike the hours all day and all night, were no ordinary timekeepers. These melodious disturbers of the peace told the farmer at the fateful hour of 5 A.M. that the time of the cuckoo had arrived and his cows were waiting to be milked.

Whatever these charming illustrations tell of the manners, morals and ways of living in the world of personal adornment applies equally in their revelations about the dressing of the well-groomed table or vanity. See to what lengths yesterday's hostess went to make sure that she displayed just the right accoutrements of the proper table setting. To be sure, there were special forks for asparagus, berry, cake, fish, fruit, lettuce, oyster and salad; special spoons for bonbon, bouillon, nut, olive, orange, radish and tomato. Bowls in every shape and size that imaginative craftsmen could conjure up were provided for fruit, gravy, candy, nut, pap, punch, salad, soup and sugar. If there was one place where the social graces put in an appropriate appearance, where years of grooming and proper breeding showed results, it was at the table. Here, well-polished silver pieces spoke the language of the four hundreds and beautifully flowered epergnes conveyed a background under correct auspices.

The secrets of the boudoir linked to woman's eternal quest for physical beauty have always provided an open sesame for makers of toiletries and articles of the dressing table. The search was once confined to a small number of women who constituted the nobility and the smart demimondaine who had the time, the money and the pressing need for preserving and accentuating their beauty. Towards the close of the nineteenth century, the search for beauty on the part of practically all women was by open proclamation. Somehow it followed that the genie of the drugstore could repair the omissions of the genes.

The beauty advice carried in the daily columns or *Godey's Lady's Book*, aside from remedies to be found in the drugstore nostrum, stressed the continuous use of comb and brush, manicure file and cuticle shaper. The general theme was simple: keep yourself in good condition and you will be attractive. Thus the many artifacts of the vanity and dresser became *de rigueur* to the well-groomed woman, a fact that manufacturers of these specialties found most profitable. A complete assortment of toilet and manicure sets, besides the usual comb and brush sets, hand mirrors, pin trays, perfume bottles and atomizers might include scissors, tweezers, nail files, buffers, etc., in great variety. For a complete beauty treatment who would dare omit all essentials if by royal decree they were the requirements?

It is axiomatic that the goods selling in a given era reveal the social and esthetic mores of that period. Because of cyclical changes due to many causes, this merchandise shows the tastes, wants and desires not merely of a handful of city dwellers but of the millions who make up the market, living in the smaller towns and on the farms throughout the land. It is a commonplace that the articles that sell in mass markets are the things that people want most. A manufacturer catering to these desires must choose between Tiffany and Woolworth, the extremes in the mercantile world, or the broad and happy medium to be found in the department stores and mail-order houses.

The styling of these products for personal or home use presents a wide range of expression. Each type of goods, fabricated of metal, wood or glass, is governed by certain technical considerations, yet in the aggregate we may define or describe a prevailing mood. The most dominant characteristic of the period is certainly the busy surface decoration, the love of floral and naturalistic detailing, the use of sentimental birds and cherubs and classically draped figures. Whether we examine the highly ornamental watchcases or elaborate table service, we note the persistence of rococo shapes and scrolls, excessive beading and incising, and the ever-present play of light and shade as the designer breaks up his surface to titillate the eye and excite with sensory delight. Many of the forms used still relate to the post-Civil War horrors and the surviving Neo-Gothic, Eastlake and Richardsonian influences.

It was this state of affairs in the decorative arts that led eventually to such a vast movement of protest and revolt by the modernists. The 1890s was a period of searching and experimentation, of restlessness and refusal to go along with the existing order. The avant-garde of the design world was disgusted with the old naturalistic formulas, the imitation of craftsmanship in shoddy machine-made wares turned out en masse to fulfill the need of the manufacturer. Out of this protest there grew a gradual return to a new order, the new art of a new time. Art Nouveau, as it was later called, was an avowed break with the tradition of the rigid nineteenth-century historical styles, a rebellion from the established order that had run its gamut.

In the thousands of illustrations included in this present survey, the author feels greatly indebted to the artists of the period under study, particularly the wood-engravers who labored so to produce the cuts shown. These unsung heroes of a bygone era afforded the only means, before the advent of the half-tone and photo-engraving, whereby merchandise of all sorts could be properly illustrated for printing and appearance in the catalogs of that day. The workrooms of these vast engraving establishments must have been teeming with hundreds bent over their tables, slaving with burin and graver under microscope to produce the delicate lines, tones and details needed to depict each subject. What an array of talent . . . what a display of genius, and what little outside comprehension and appreciation of the tremendously arduous tasks involved. To them, we give humble thanks.

C. P. H.

New York, N.Y.
September 1967

All engravings and their accompanying captions have been reproduced from the original old catalogs, which explains variant spellings and an occasional odd bit of type.

CONTENTS

THE PLATES

Solid Silver Ware

BON-BON DISHES

Fine Silver Plated Hollow Ware

BON-BON BASKETS

NUT, BERRY AND SALAD BOWLS

Nut Bowl.

Nut or Berry Bowl.

Nut or Berry Bowl.

Nut or Salad Bowl.

Nut or Berry Bowl.

Nut or Berry Bowl.

Fine Silver Plated Hollow Ware

CAKE BASKETS

CAKE BASKETS

Fine Silver Plated Hollow Ware
BERRY OR FRUIT DISHES

BERRY OR FRUIT DISHES

Genuine American Cut Glassware

Handy Nappy (Round.)

Handy Nappy (3 Cornered).

Punch Bowl.

Salad Bowl.

Salad Bowl.

Water Pitcher.

Carafe or Water Bottle.

Carafe or Water Bottle.

Carafe or Water Bottle.

Water Set, Silver Plated Tray.

Tankard Jug.

Celery Stand.

Spoon Holder.

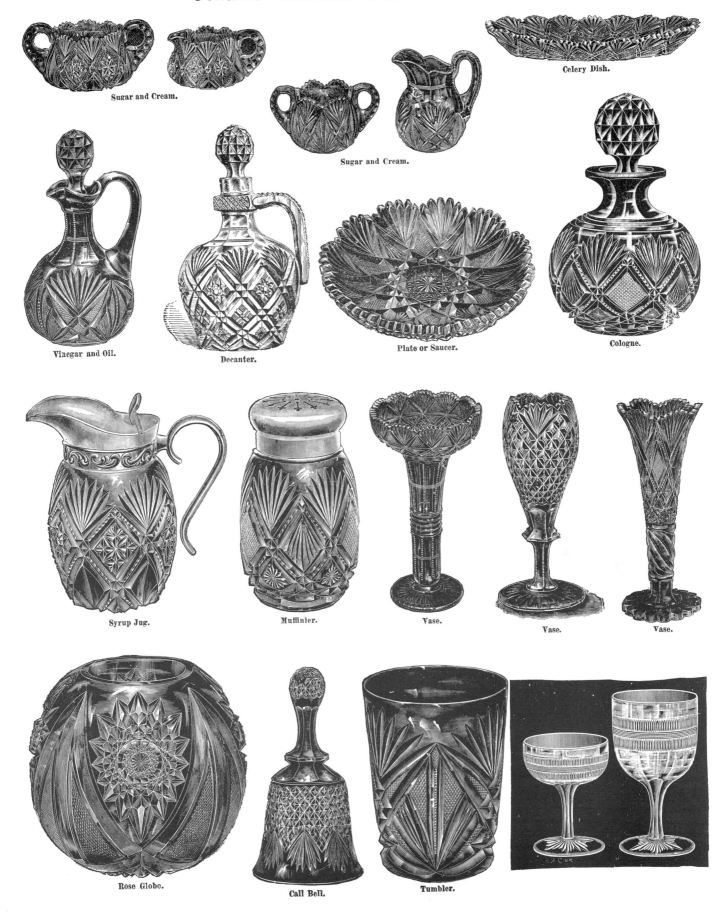

Sugar and Cream.

Sugar and Cream.

Celery Dish.

Vinegar and Oil.

Decanter.

Plate or Saucer.

Cologne.

Syrup Jug.

Muffinier.

Vase.

Vase.

Vase.

Rose Globe.

Call Bell.

Tumbler.

Fine Silver Plated Hollow Ware

TEA KETTLES, PERCOLATORS, ETC.

Tea or Coffee Kettle.

Tea or Coffee Kettle.

Swinging Tea or Coffee Kettle.

Coffee Percolator.

Urn.

Fine Silver Plated Hollow Ware

TEA SETS

Fine Silver Plated Hollow Ware

TEA SETS

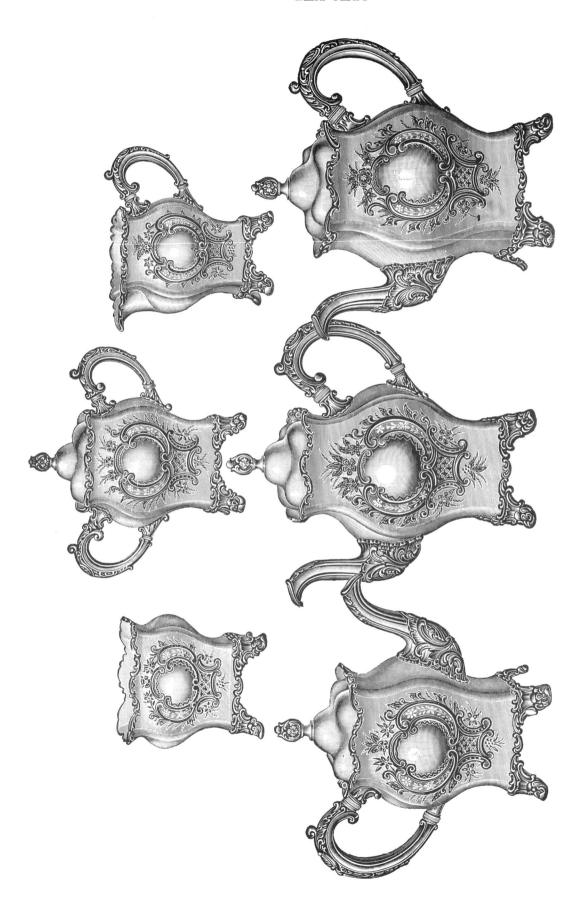

TEA SETS

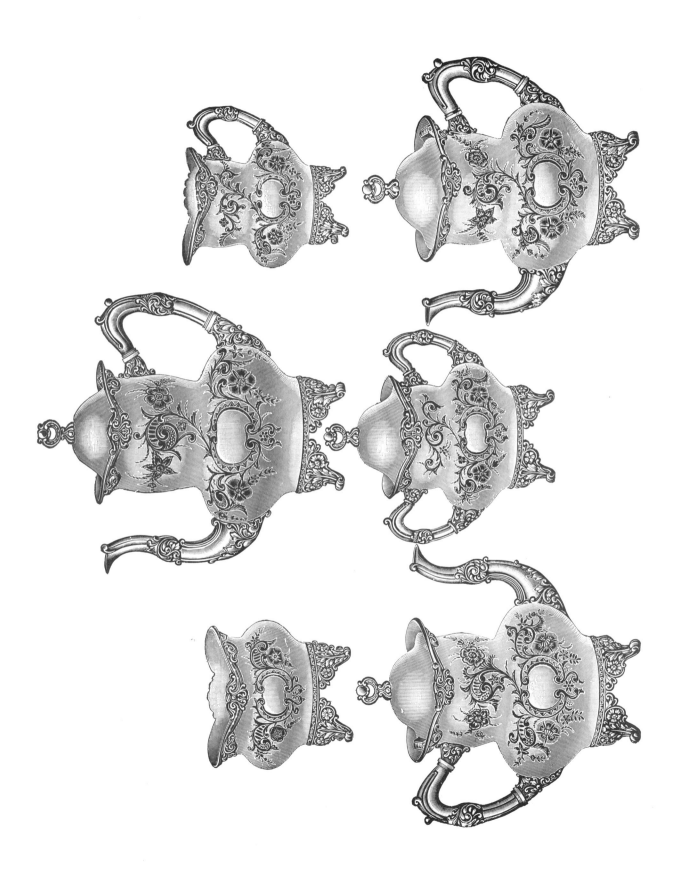

Silver Plated Hollow Ware

TEA SETS

SPOON HOLDER.

CREAM PITCHER.

SUGAR BOWL.

COFFEE POT.

COFFEE POT.

SUGAR BOWL.

SPOON HOLDER.

CREAM PITCHER.

CREAM PITCHER.

SPOON HOLDER.

SUGAR BOWL.

COFFEE POT.

Fine Silver Plated Hollow Ware

TEA SETS

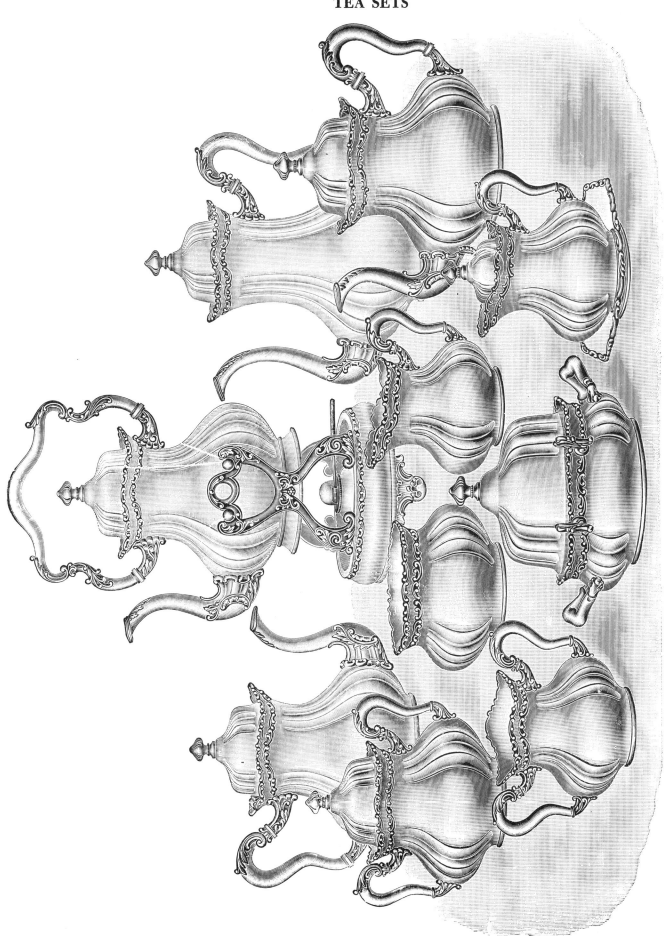

Fine Silver Plated Hollow Ware

COFFEE AND TETE-A-TETE SETS

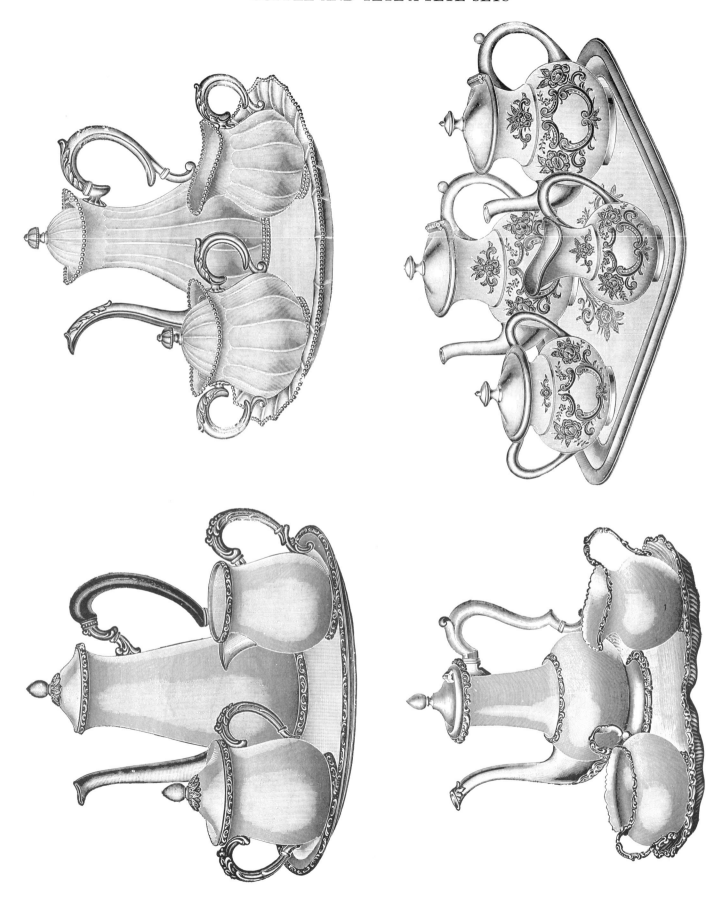

Fine Silver Plated Hollow Ware

WATER PITCHERS

Fine Silver Plated Hollow Ware

TILTING WATER SETS

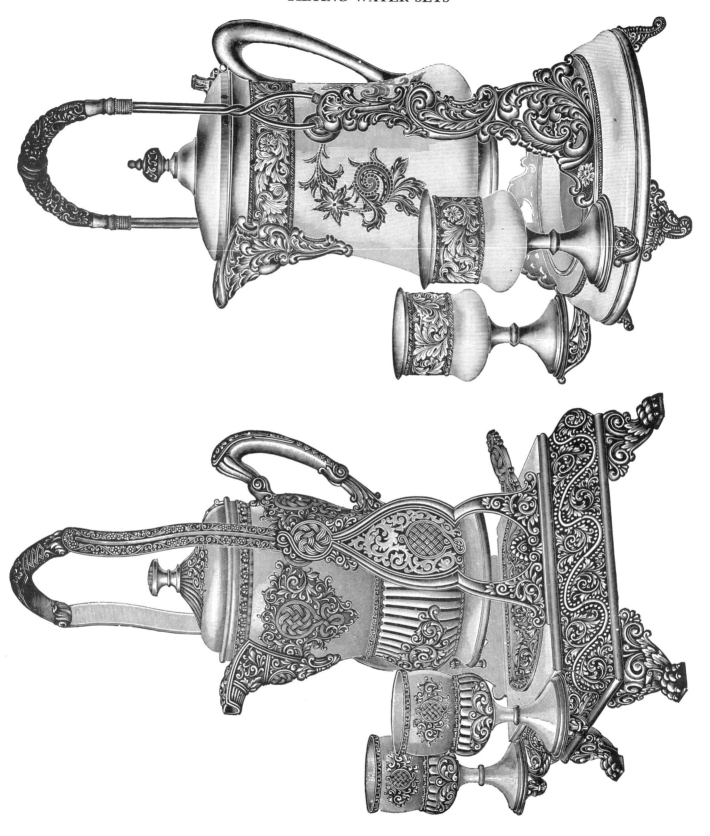

TILTING WATER SETS

Fine Silver Plated Hollow Ware

TILTING WATER SETS

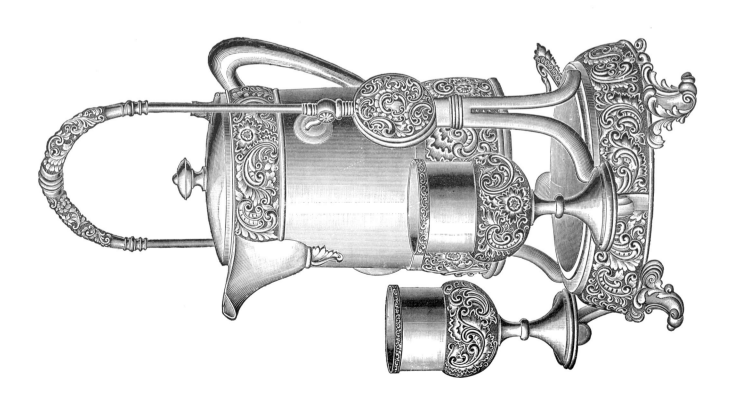

Silver Plated Hollow Ware.

TILTING WATER SETS

Fine Silver Plated Hollow Ware

WATER SETS

Water Set.

Water Pitcher.

Water Set.

Water Pitcher.

DESSERT SETS

Cream Pitcher.

Cream Pitcher.

Cream Pitcher.

Spoon Holder.

Spoon Holder.

Spoon Holder.

Sugar Bowl.

Sugar Bowl.

Sugar Bowl.

Fine Silver Plated Hollow Ware

CHILDREN'S CUPS

Silver Plated Hollow Ware

BUTTER DISH

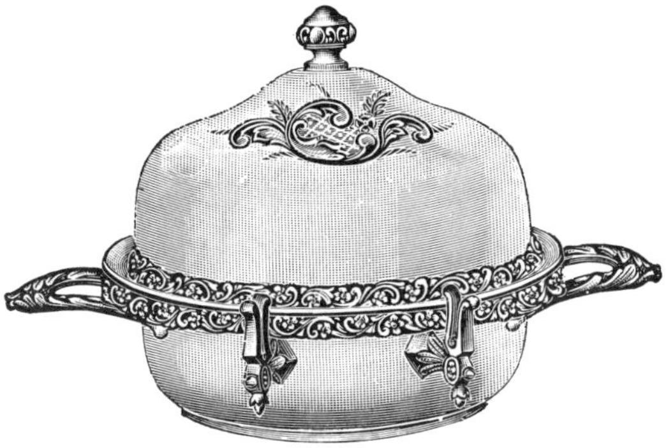

BUTTER DISH.

BUTTER DISH.

FRUIT OR BERRY DISH.

BUTTER DISH.

FRUIT OR BERRY DISH.

FRUIT OR BERRY DISH

FRUIT OR BERRY DISH.

Fine Silver Plated Hollow Ware

BUTTER DISHES

Fine Silver Plated Hollow Ware

BUTTER DISHES

Fine Silver Plated Hollow Ware
PICKLE CASTERS WITH TONGS

SYRUP CUPS

Fine Silver Plated Hollow Ware
SUGAR BOWLS, CONDENSED MILK HOLDERS, ETC.

Condensed Milk Holder.

Pap Bowl and Plate.

Pap Bowl and Plate.

Gravy Boat.

Biscuit Jar.

Mustard.

Collapsing Cup.

Mustard.

Condensed Milk Holder.

Sugar Bowl and Spoon Holder Combined.

Chocolate Pot.

Fine Silver Plated Hollow Ware

SUGAR SIFTERS, TEA CADDY, BALLS, ETC.

Tea Strainer with Handle.

Tea Ball.

Tea Strainer.

Sugar Sifter

Sugar Sifter.

Sugar Sifter.

Sugar Sifter.

Silver Plated Hollow Ware
SYRUPS, PITCHERS, ETC.

Syrup.

Sugar and Spoon Holder, Combined.

Syrup, with Plate.

Baking Dish.

Berry or Fruit Dish.

Waiter.

Water Pitcher.

Silver Plated Hollow Ware
CHILD'S CUPS, SHAVING CUPS, ETC.

CHILD'S CUP.

PEN WIPER.

CALENDAR.

FERN DISH.

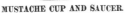

MUSTACHE CUP AND SAUCER.

CHILD'S CUP.

CHILD'S CUP.

BON-BON BASKET.

ORANGE CUP.

SHAVING CUP AND BRUSH.

FERN DISH.

CHILD'S CUP.

Fine Silver Plated Hollow Ware

DINNER CASTERS

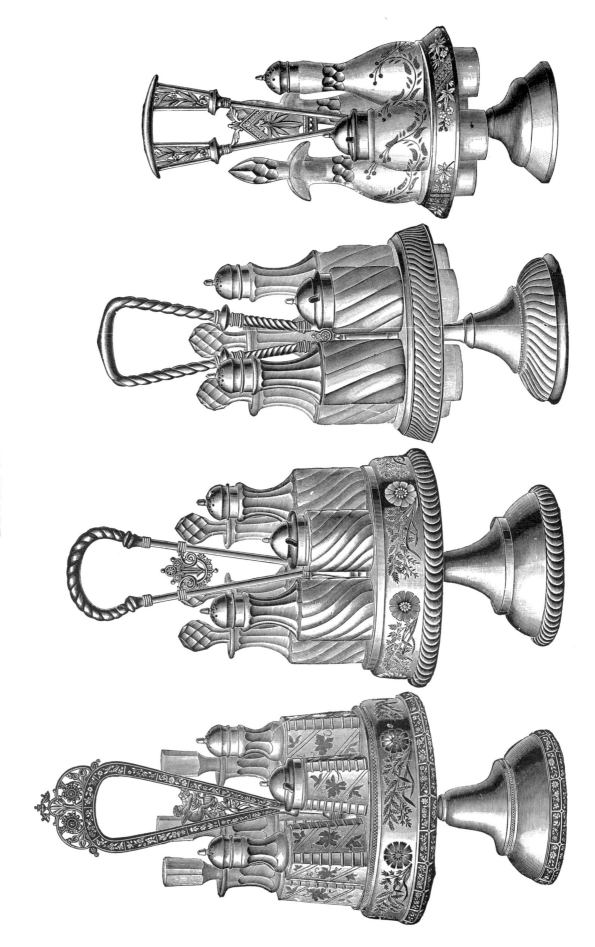

BREAKFAST CASTERS

Silver Plated Hollow Ware

CASTERS AND CELERY BOAT

CELERY BOAT.

SALAD CASTER.

CASTER.

CASTER.

CASTER.

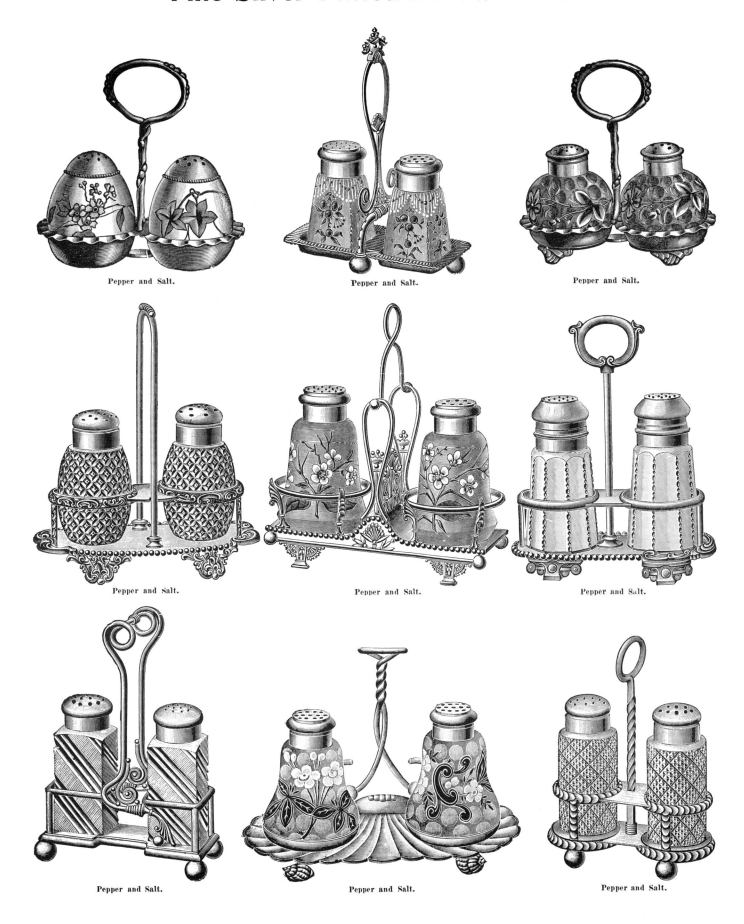

Pepper and Salt.

Pepper and Salt.

Pepper and Salt.

Pepper and Salt.

Pepper and Salt.

Pepper and Salt.

Pepper and Salt.

Pepper and Salt.

Pepper and Salt.

FINE SILVER PLATED HOLLOW WARE

INDIVIDUAL SALTS AND PEPPERS

Salt or Pepper.

Salt or Pepper.

Salt or Pepper.

Salt or Pepper.

Salt or Pepper.

Salt or Pepper.

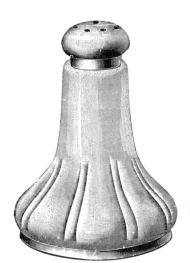
Salt or Pepper.

Salt or Pepper.

Salt or Pepper.

Salt or Pepper.

Salt or Pepper.

Salt or Pepper.

Salt or Pepper.

Salt or Pepper.

Salt or Pepper.

SALT AND LUNCH SETS

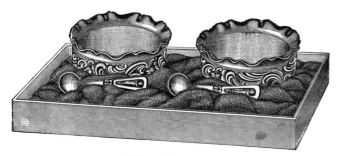

Salts and Spoons.

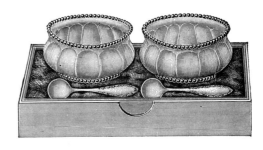

Salts and Spoons.

Lunch Set.

Salts and Spoons.

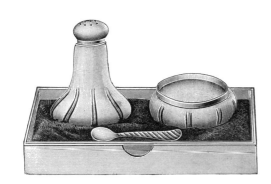

Lunch Set.

Lunch Set.

Lunch Set.

Lunch Set.

Fine Silver Plated Hollow Ware

BAKING DISHES

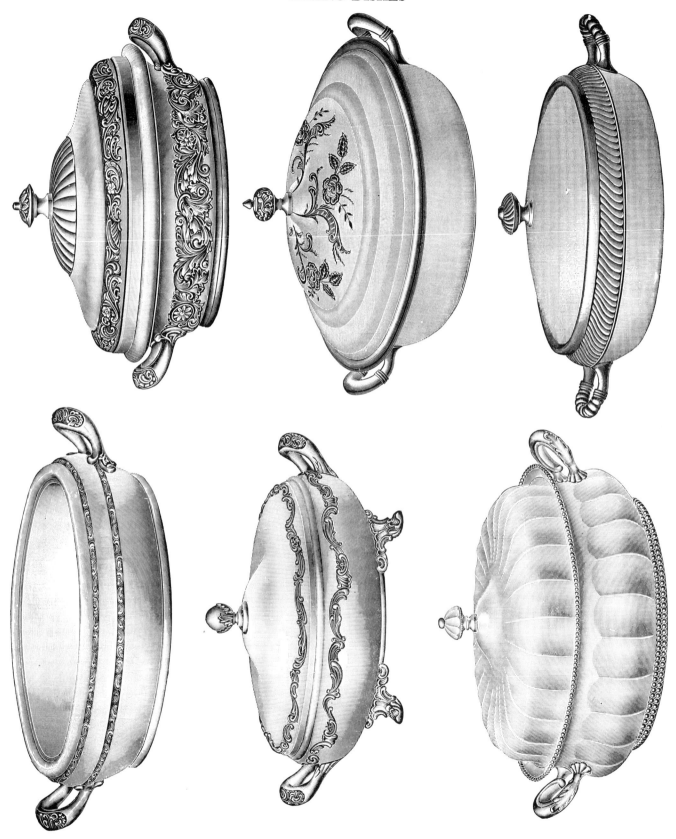

...GNE AND TOOTH PICK OR MATCH HOLDERS

Epergne.

Match or Tooth Pick Holder.

Match or Tooth Pick Holder.

Match or Tooth Pick Holder.

Match or Tooth Pick Holder.

Match or Tooth Pick Holder.

Solid Silver Ware

SALTS, PEPPERS, BUTTER PLATES, ETC.

Salt Cellar.

Salt Cellar.

Salt or Pepper.

Salt or Pepper.

Salt Cellar.

Individual Butter Plate.

Individual Butter Plate.

Individual Butter Plate.

Salt Cellar.

Salt Cellar.

Salt Cellar.

Tea Strainer.

Tea Strainer.

Tea Strainer.

Tea Ball.

Fine Silver Plated Hollow Ware

CRUMB TRAYS AND SCRAPERS

Fine Silver Plated Hollow Ware

WINE CASTER, COOLERS, ETC.

Ice Tub.

Bar Pitcher.

Ice Tub.

Wine Cooler.

Wine Caster.

Wine Cooler.

BAR GOODS

Liquor Mixer, Plain.

Bar Jigger.

Knife Rest.

Glass Holder,

Knife Rest

Bottle Holder (for Quart Bottle).

Knife Rest, Chased

Bottle Holder,

Corkscrew

Knife Rest

Patent Corkscrew

Glass Holder

Solid Silver Ware

NAPKIN RINGS

Fine Silver Plated Hollow Ware

NAPKIN RINGS

Lettuce Fork. Cold Meat or Salad Fork. Cold Meat or Cake Fork. Cold Meat or Salad Fork. Lettuce Fork.

Solid Silver Ware

FISH AND ICE CREAM KNIVES

Fish Knife.

Ice Cream Slicer.

Ice Cream Slicer.

Solid Silver Ware

BERRY AND SALAD SPOONS

Berry and Salad Spoon.   Berry or Salad Spoon.   Berry or Salad Spoon.   Berry or Salad Spoon.

Solid Silver Ware

BON-BON SPOONS, ETC.

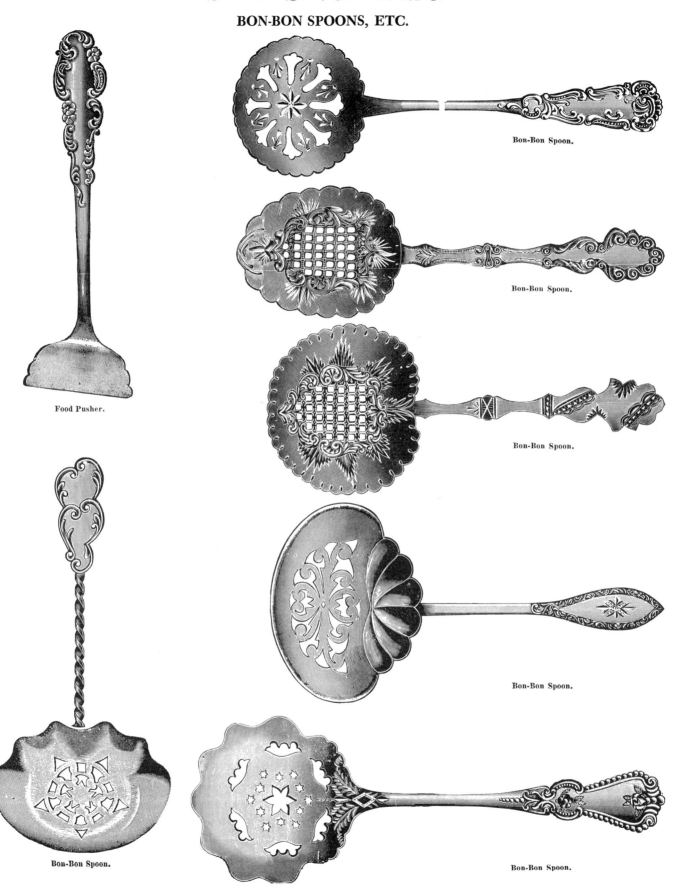

Food Pusher.

Bon-Bon Spoon.

Bon-Bon Spoon.

Bon-Bon Spoon.

Bon-Bon Spoon.

Bon-Bon Spoon.

Bon-Bon Spoon.

JELLY, PRESERVE AND PEA SPOONS, AND JELLY TROWELS

Jelly Trowel.

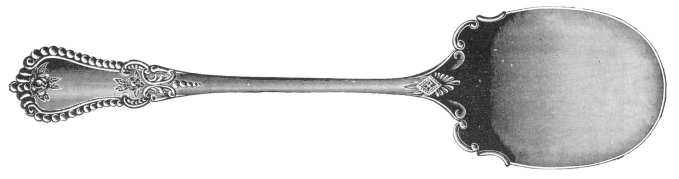

Jelly or Preserve Spoon.

Jelly or Preserve Spoon.

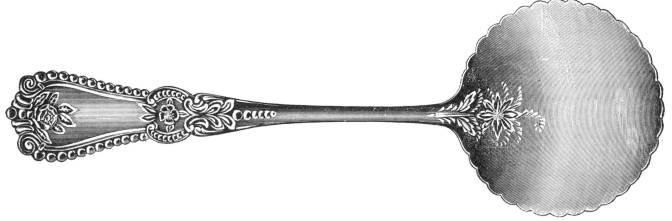

Pea Spoon.

Solid Silver Ware

SUGAR SHELLS

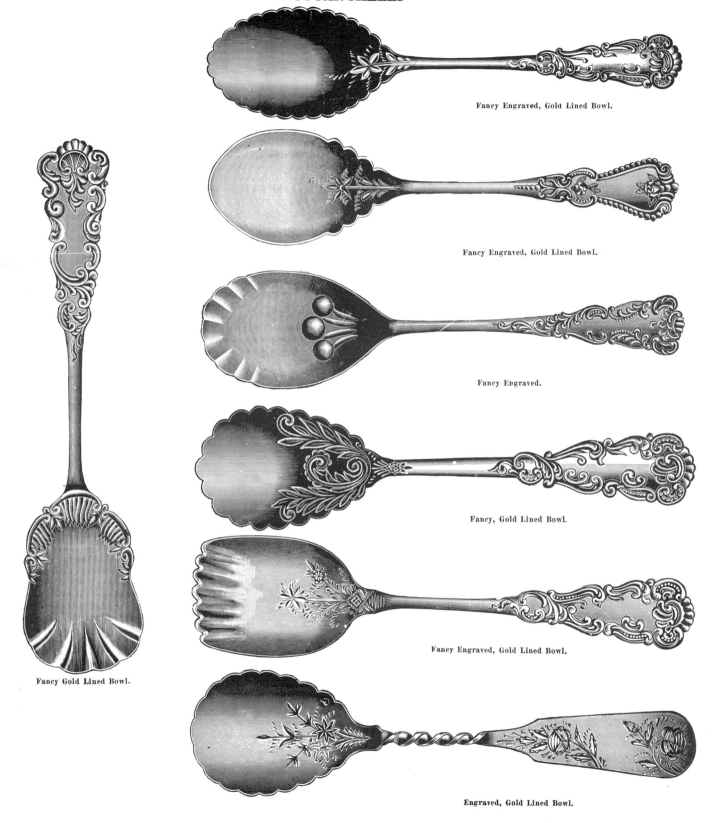

Fancy Engraved, Gold Lined Bowl.

Fancy Engraved, Gold Lined Bowl.

Fancy Engraved.

Fancy Gold Lined Bowl.

Fancy, Gold Lined Bowl.

Fancy Engraved, Gold Lined Bowl.

Engraved, Gold Lined Bowl.

Solid Silver Ware

TOMATO, CUCUMBER AND ICE CREAM FORKS

Ice Cream Fork.

Cheese Scoop.

Cheese Scoop.

Ice Cream Fork.

Tomato Fork.

Cucumber Fork.

Tomato Fork.

Solid Silver Ware

COFFEE AND SOUVENIR SPOONS

Solid Silver Ware

BERRY, OYSTER FORKS, ETC.

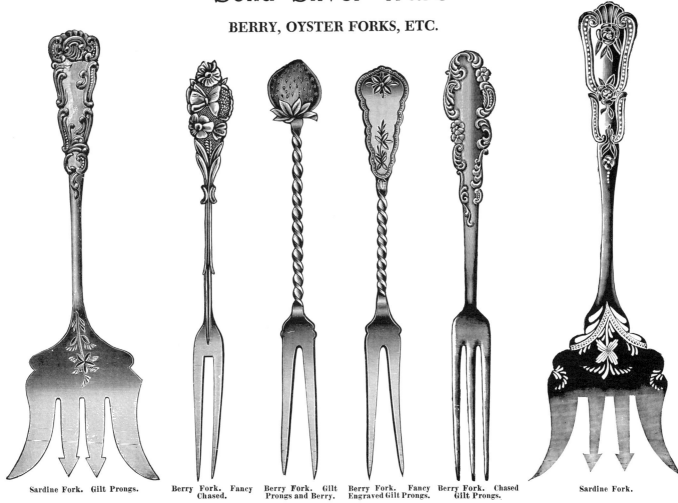

Sardine Fork. Gilt Prongs.

Berry Fork. Fancy Chased.

Berry Fork. Gilt Prongs and Berry.

Berry Fork. Fancy Engraved Gilt Prongs.

Berry Fork. Chased Gilt Prongs.

Sardine Fork.

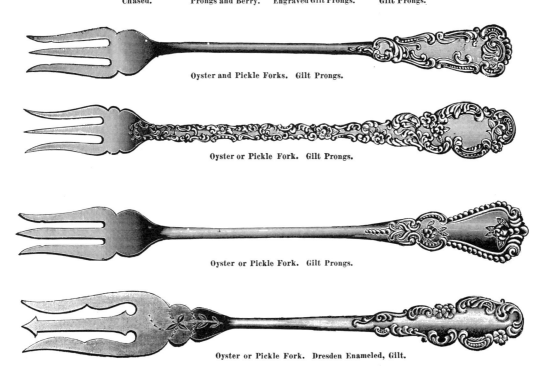

Oyster and Pickle Forks. Gilt Prongs.

Oyster or Pickle Fork. Gilt Prongs.

Oyster or Pickle Fork. Gilt Prongs.

Oyster or Pickle Fork. Dresden Enameled, Gilt.

Fine Silver Plated Flat Ware

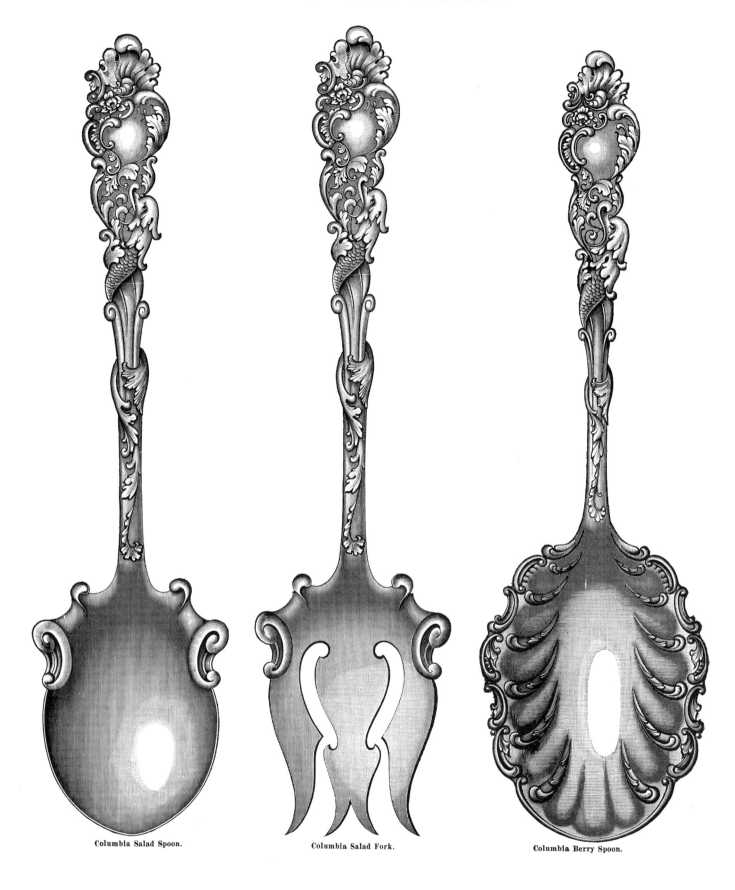

Columbia Salad Spoon.

Columbia Salad Fork.

Columbia Berry Spoon.

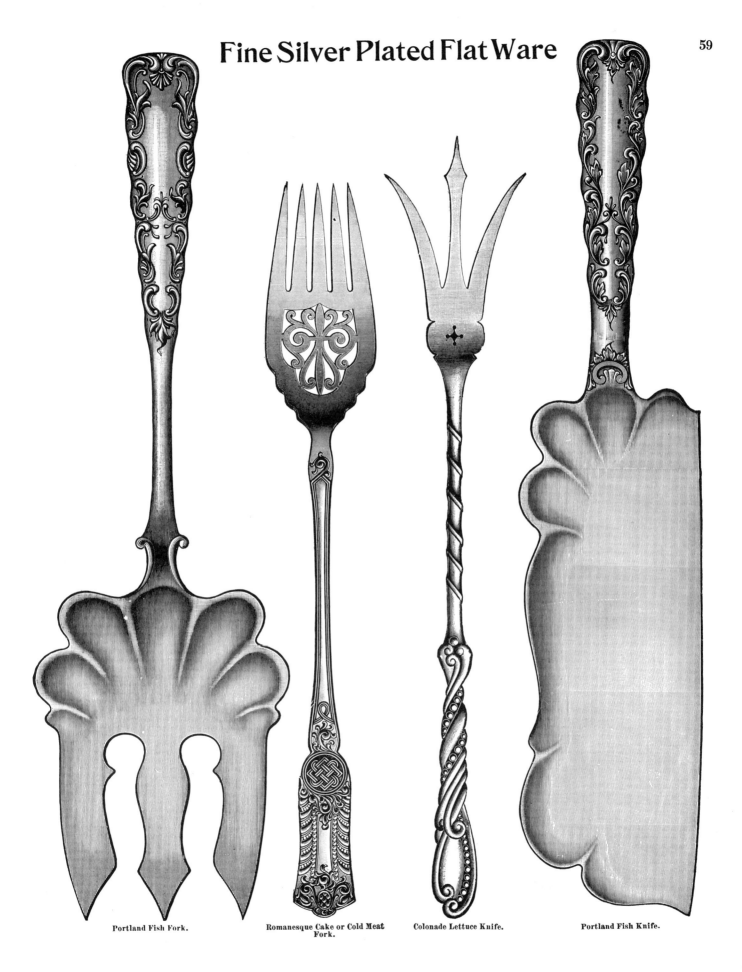

Portland Fish Fork.

Romanesque Cake or Cold Meat Fork.

Colonade Lettuce Knife.

Portland Fish Knife.

Fine Silver Plated Flat Ware

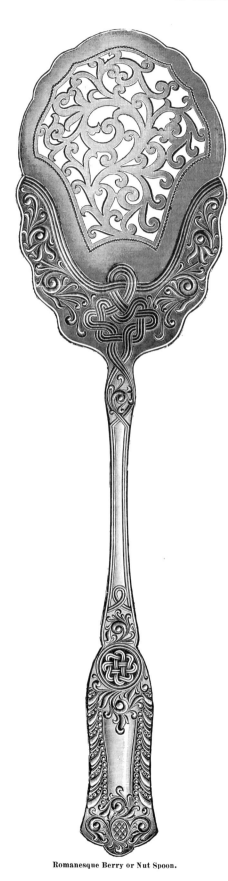

Romanesque Berry or Nut Spoon.

Length of Blade, 5¼ Inches.

Portland Pie Server.

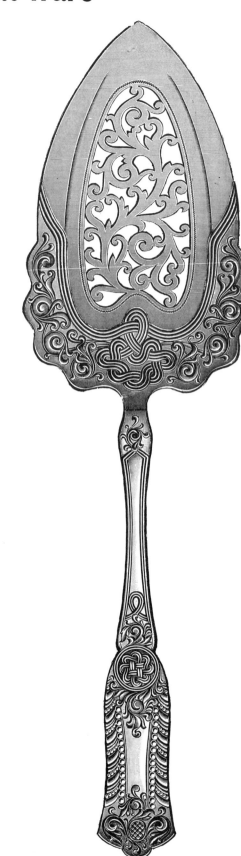

Romanesque Pie Knife.

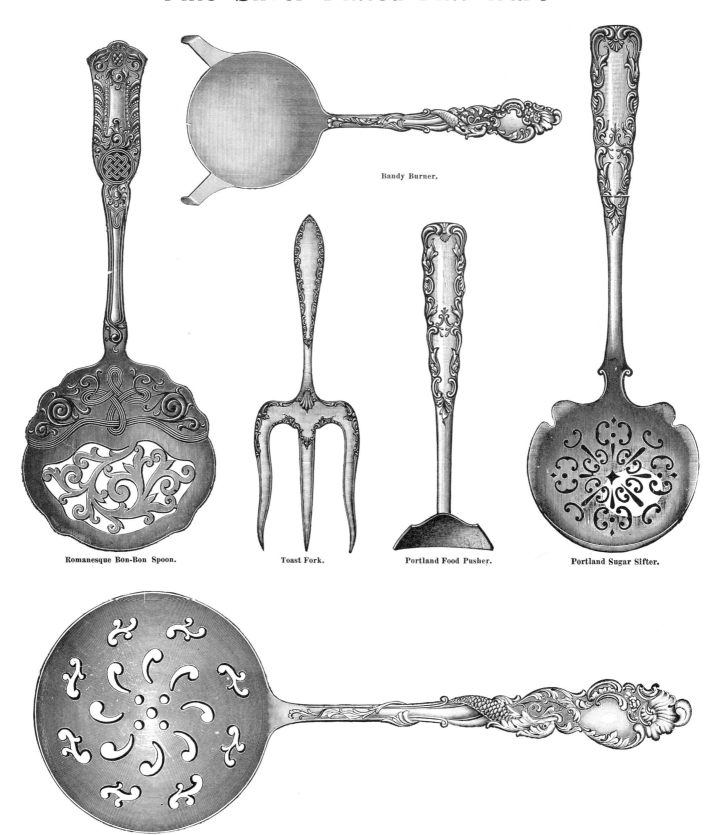

Bandy Burner.

Romanesque Bon-Bon Spoon.

Toast Fork.

Portland Food Pusher.

Portland Sugar Sifter.

Columbia Tomato and Cucumber Server.

COLUMBIA Sugar Shell.

LOTUS Sugar Shell.

ROMANESQUE Butter Spreader.

COLUMBIA Butter Spreader.

VESTA Butter Knife.

COLUMBIA Butter Knife.

"Majestic" Butter Knife.

Shell Butter Knife.

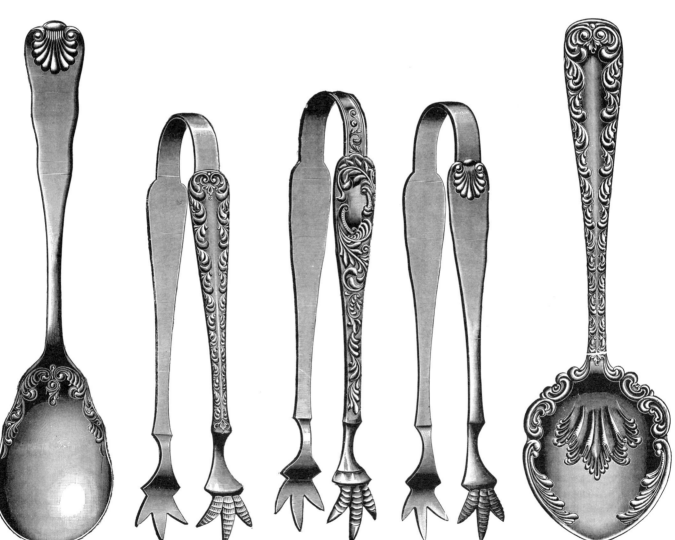

| Shell Sugar Shell. | Majestic Sugar Tong. | Monarch Sugar Tong. | Shell Sugar Tong. | Majestic Sugar Shell. |

Fine Silver Plated Flat Ware

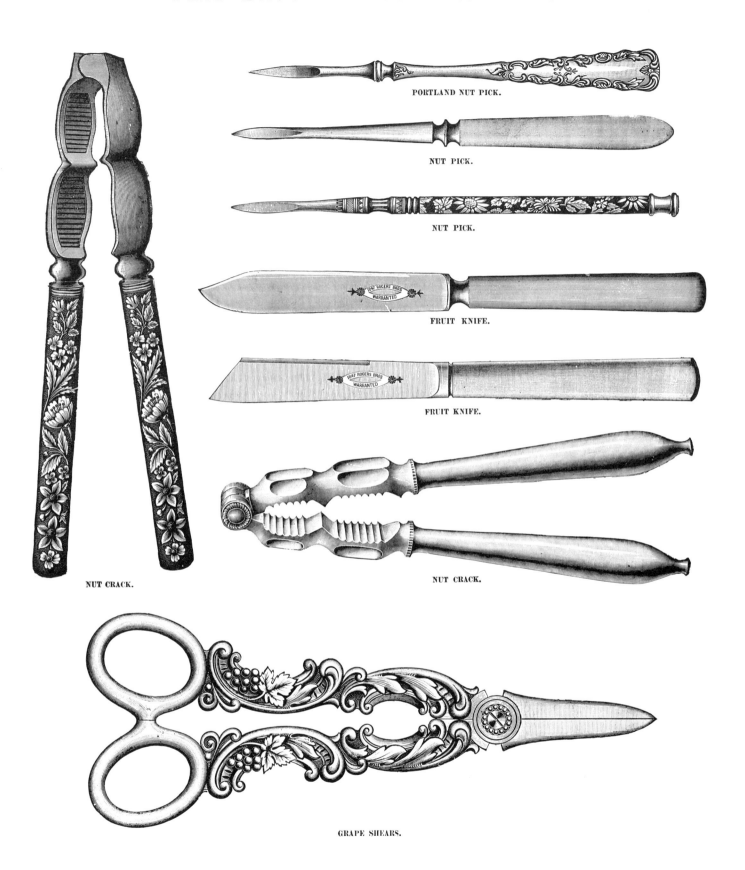

PORTLAND NUT PICK.

NUT PICK.

NUT PICK.

FRUIT KNIFE.

FRUIT KNIFE.

NUT CRACK.

NUT CRACK.

GRAPE SHEARS.

Fine Table Cutlery
KNIVES AND NUT PICKS

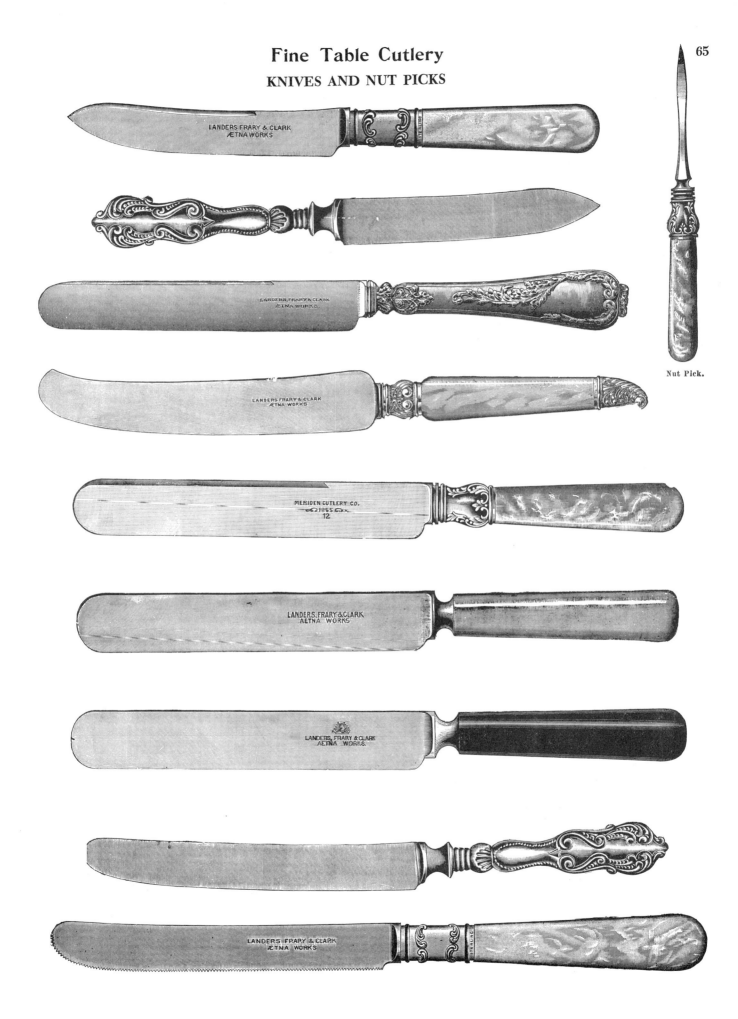

Nut Pick.

Fine Table Cutlery

CARVING SET

CARVING SETS, IN SATIN LINED BOXES

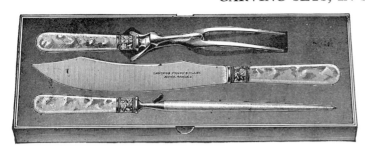 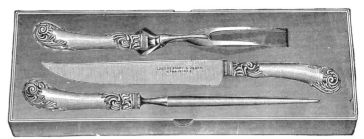

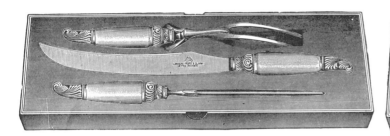 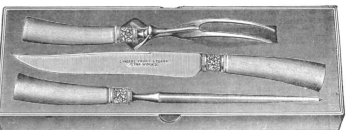

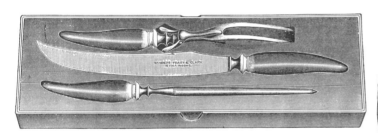 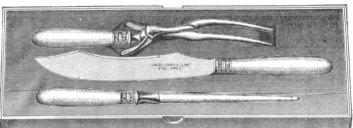

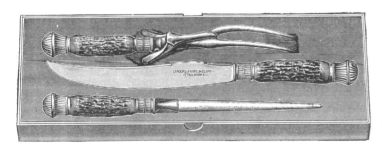 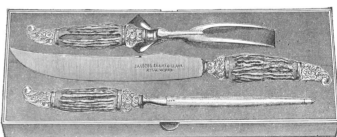

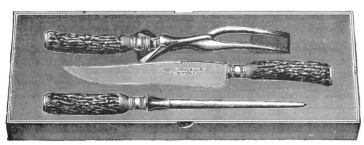 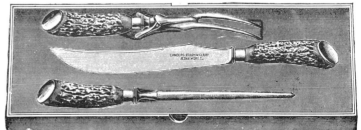

Fine Silver Plated Flat Ware

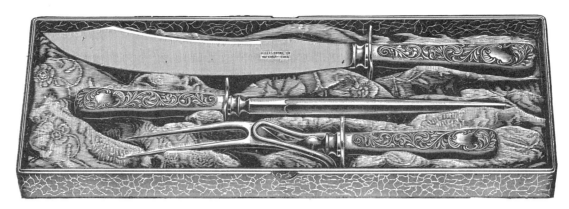

Monarch Carving Set.

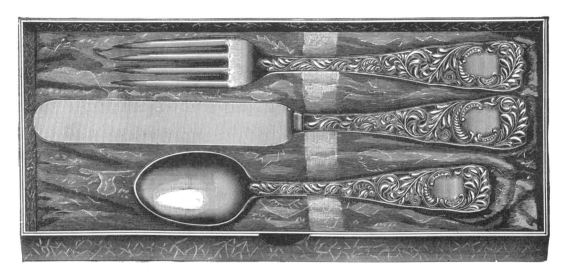

Monarch Child's Set.

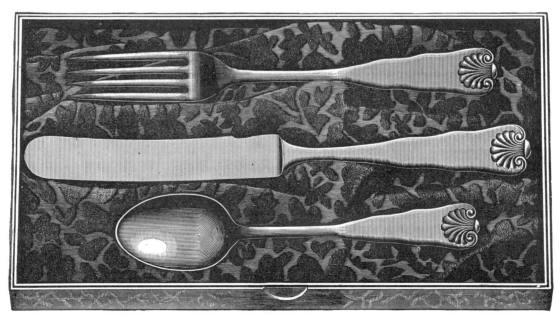

Shell Child's Set.

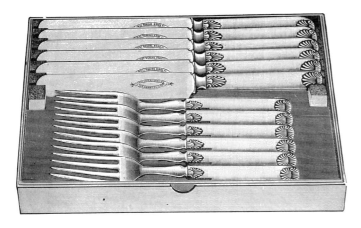

Six Shell Medium Knives and Six Forks.

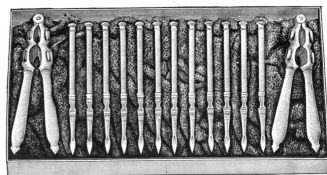

Twelve Nut Pickers and Two Cracks.

Housekeepers' Outfit Complete.

Fine Art Metal Goods

FERN DISHES, FLASKS, ETC.

Flask.

Flask.

Flask.

Flask.

Flower Pot.

Flower Pot.

Fern Dish.

Fern Dish.

Fern Dish.

Fine Silver Plated Hollow Ware

COMMUNION WARE, CHAFING DISHES, ETC.

Individual Communion Set.

Pocket Communion Set.

Individual Communion Set.

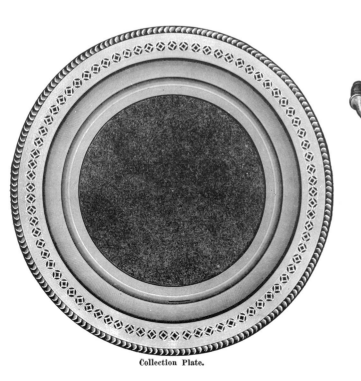

Collection Plate.

Chafing Dish. (Nickel Silver.)

CANDELABRUM AND CANDLESTICKS

Candlestick.

Candlestick.

Candlestick.

Candlestick.

Candlestick.

Candlestick.

Candelabrum.

Candlestick.

Fine Silver Plated Hollow Ware

CALENDARS, THERMOMETERS AND BLOTTERS

Thermometer.

Calendar.

Calendar.

Blotter.

Stationery Holder and Calendar.

Blotter and Calendar Combined.

Thermometer.

Daily Calendar.

Perpetual Calendar.

Solid Silver Ware

PICTURE FRAMES

Fine Silver Plated Hollow Ware

SMOKING SETS, CIGAR AND HOLDERS

Smoking Set.

Smokers' Set.

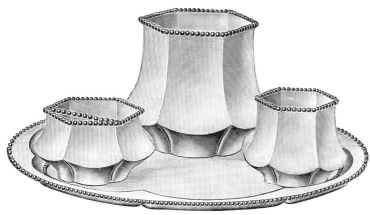

Smoking Set.

Cigar and Ash Holder.

Smoking Set.

Cigar and Ash Holder.

Fine Silver Plated Hollow Ware

TRINKET, GLOVE AND HANDKERCHIEF BOXES, ETC.

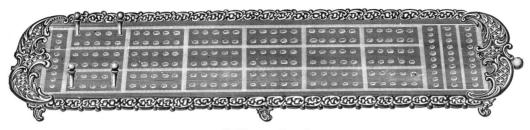

Cribbage Board.

Glove Box.

Handkerchief Box.

Hair Pin Box.

Trinket Box.

Trinket Box.

Trinket Box.

Trinket Box.

Fine Silver Plated Hollow Ware

TRINKET TRAYS AND CELERY BOAT

Ring Stand.

Ring Stand.

Ring Stand.

Trinket Tray.

Trinket Tray.

Trinket Tray.

Trinket Tray.

Trinket Tray.

Trinket Tray.

Trinket Tray.

Trinket Tray.

CARD RECEIVERS

Fine Silver Plated Hollow Ware

JEWEL CASKETS

Solid Silver Ware

PIN OR TRINKET TRAYS

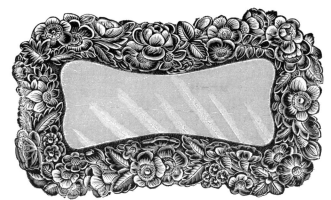

Pin or Trinket Tray.

Pin or Trinket Tray.

Pin Tray.

Pin or Trinket Tray.

Pin or Trinket Tray.

Pin or Trinket Tray.

Pin or Trinket Tray.

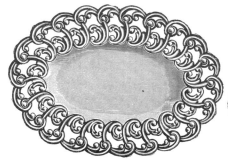

Pin Tray.

Pin or Trinket Tray.

Fine Silver Plated Hollow Ware

PRIZE CUPS AND FIRE TRUMPETS

Firemen's Trumpet.

Prize Cup.

Prize Cup.

Fine Silver Plated Hollow Ware

PRIZE CUPS

Fine Gold Pens

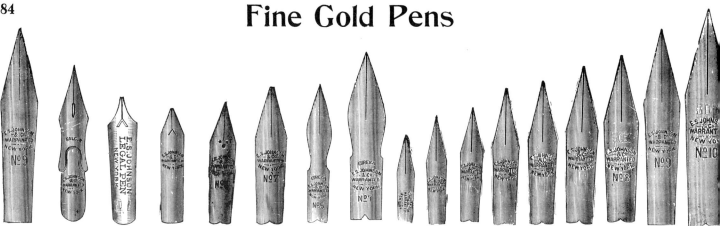

14 K. Solid Gold Plain or Chased Twist Pen Holder.

Sterling Silver Chased Pen Holder.

Sterling Silver Chased Pen Holder.

Sterling Silver Chased, Indian or Owl Center Pen Holder.

Sterling Silver Assorted Twist or Fluted Pen Holder.

Rolled Gold Plate Chased Pen Holder.

Rolled Gold Plated Screw Pen Holder and Pencil.

Rolled Gold Plate Enameled Screw Pen Holder and Pencil.

Rolled Gold Plate Ebony Telescopic Pocket Pen Holder.

Fine White Pearl Desk Holder, Rolled Gold Plate Nose.

Fine White Rustic Pearl Holder, Rolled Gold Plate Nose.

Fine White Pearl Slide Holder, Rolled Gold Plate Mounting.

Fine White Pearl Rustic Slide Holder, Rolled Gold Plate Mounting.

Fine White Twist Pearl Desk Holder, Rolled Gold Plate Nose.

Fine Ivory Desk Holder, Rolled Gold Plate Nose.

Fine Ebony Desk Holder, Rolled Gold Plate Nose.

Black Celluloid Slide Pocket Holder and Pencil, Rolled Gold Plate Mountings.

Black Celluloid Reversible Holder, Rolled Gold Plate Nose.

Rolled Gold Plate Telescopic Pocket Holder and Pencil.

Gold, Rolled Gold Plate and Silver
PENCIL CHARMS, TOOTH PICKS AND EAR SPOONS

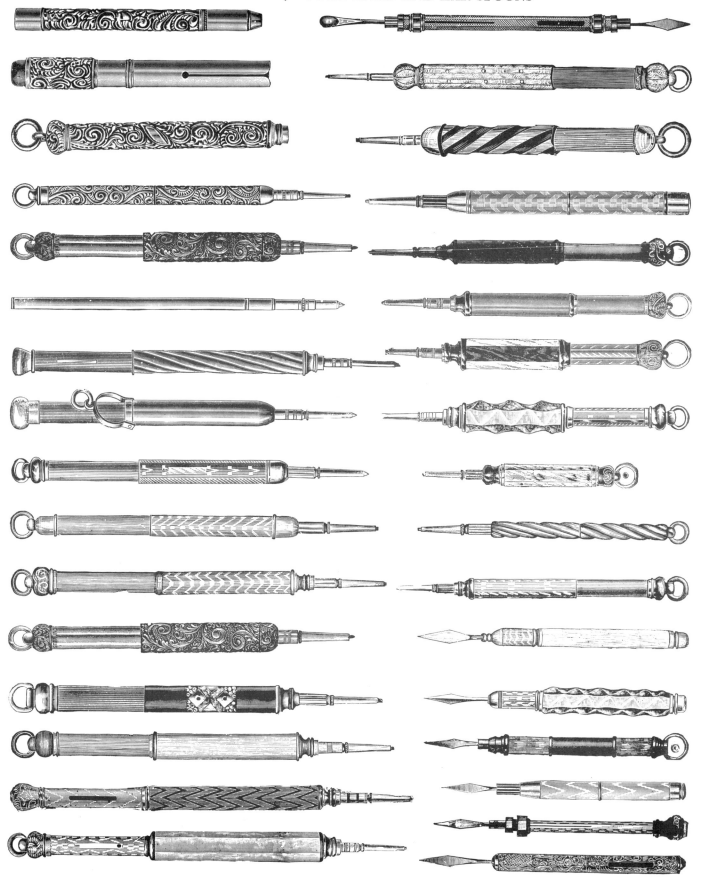

Sterling Silver Pen Holder and Pencil Outfit

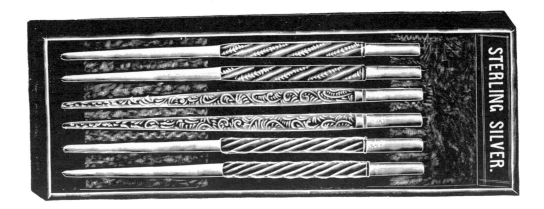

Fine Rolled Gold Plate Pencil Outfit.

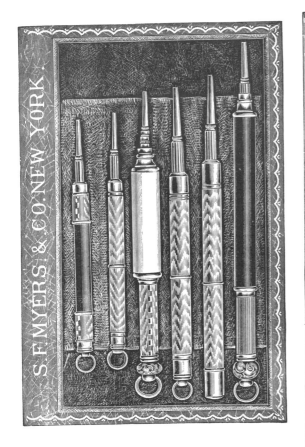

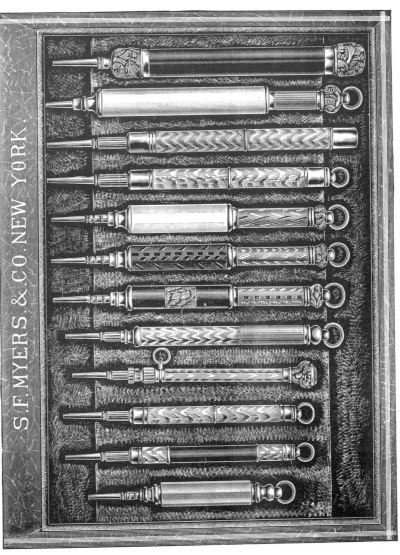

Silver Plated Hollow Ware

Jewel Case.

Pin or Trinket Tray.

Candle Stick.

Ink Stand.

Stamp and Pen Tray.

Nick-Nack Cabinet.

Jewel Case.

Ink Stand.

Ink Stand.

Ink Stand.

Jewel Case.

Spool Box.

Trinket Cabinet.

Card or Bon-Bon Basket.

Curling Iron Set.

Calendar.

Calendar.

Fine Silver Plated Hollow Ware

CIGAR BOXES AND LAMPS

Cigar Box.

Smoking Set.

Cigar Box.

Cigar Box.

Cigar Lamp.

Cigar Lamp.

Cigar Box.

Fine Silver Plated Hollow Ware

CALL BELLS

Solid Silver Ware

MATCH SAFES

Solid Silver Ware

CHILD'S CUPS, SHAVING CUPS, ETC.

Child's Cup.

Child's Cup.

Shaving Brush.

Shaving Set.

Child's Cup.

Child's Cup.

Shaving Stick, Soap Box.

Shaving Cup.

LAVATORY SETS

Tooth Brush Box.

Sponge Bowl.

Puff Box.

Cup.

Soap Box.

Tooth Powder Box.

Cup.

Tooth Brush Holder.

Fine Silver Plated Hollow Ware
TOILET SETS, VASES AND VASELINE HOLDER

Chased Vaseline Holder

Toilet Set.

Solid Silver Ware

MIRRORS, ETC.

Nail Brush.

Traveling Mirror.

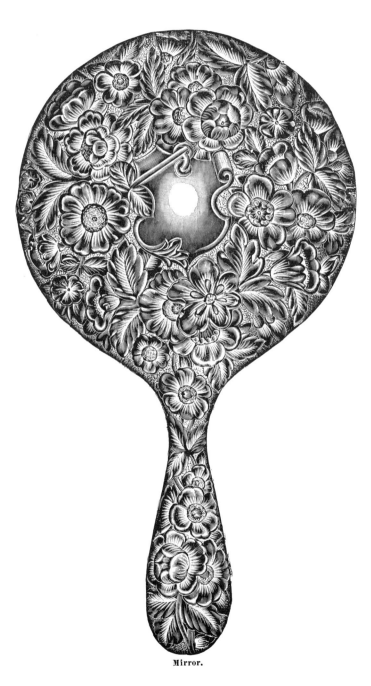

Mirror.

Mirror.

Solid Silver Ware

TOILET ARTICLES

Velvet Brush.

Comb.

Cloth Brush.

Hair Brush.

Hat Brush.

Military Brush.

Solid Silver Ware

TOILET ARTICLES

Hair Brush.

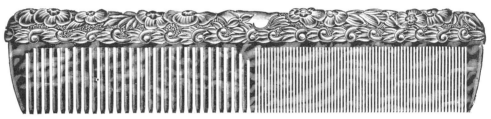

Cloth Brush.

Comb.

Velvet Brush.

Hat Brush.

Hat Brush.

Military Brush.

Fine Silver Plated Hollow Ware

Whisk Broom.

Military Brush.

Bonnet Brush.

Hand Mirror.

Mustache or Nail Brush.

Hair Brush.

Hat Brush.

Comb.

Cloth Brush.

Velvet Brush.

Solid Silver Ware

BONNET AND WHISK BROOMS

Bonnet Brush.

Bonnet Brush.

Bonnet Brush.

Whisk Broom.

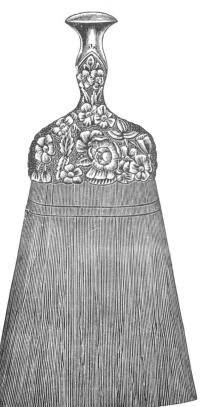

Whisk Broom.

Whisk Broom.

Solid Silver Novelties

MANICURE ARTICLES

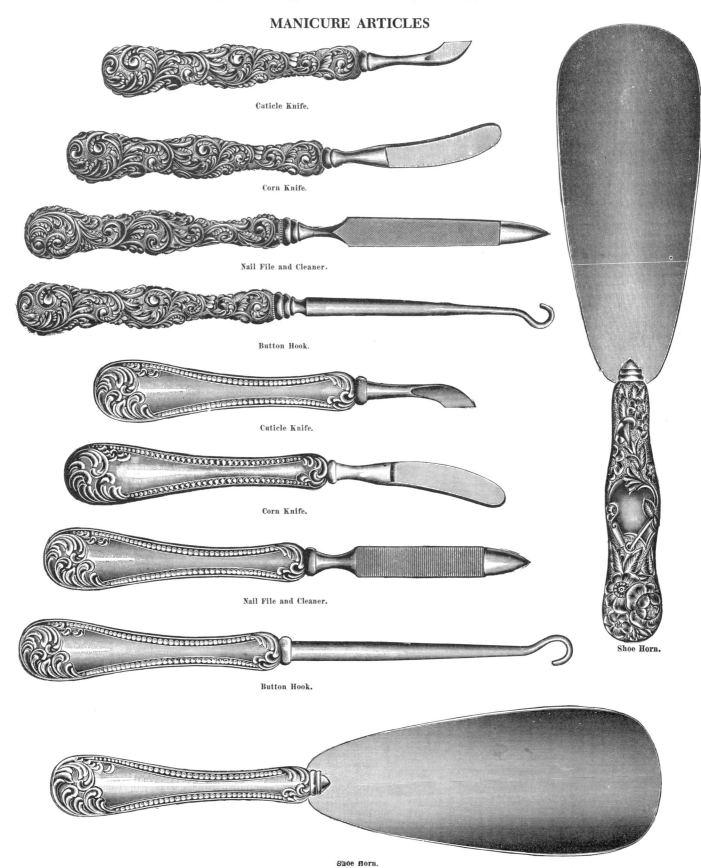

Caticle Knife.

Corn Knife.

Nail File and Cleaner.

Button Hook.

Cuticle Knife.

Corn Knife.

Nail File and Cleaner.

Button Hook.

Shoe Horn.

Shoe Horn.

MANICURE ARTICLES

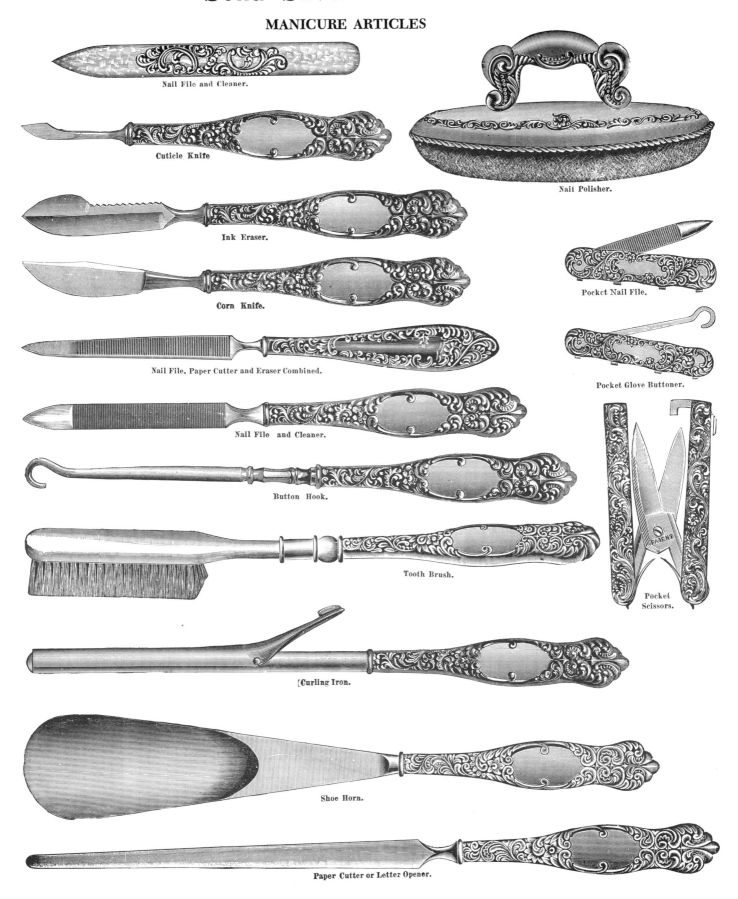

Nail File and Cleaner.

Cuticle Knife

Nail Polisher.

Ink Eraser.

Corn Knife.

Pocket Nail File.

Nail File, Paper Cutter and Eraser Combined.

Nail File and Cleaner.

Pocket Glove Buttoner.

Button Hook.

Tooth Brush.

Pocket Scissors.

[Curling Iron.

Shoe Horn.

Paper Cutter or Letter Opener.

Solid Silver Ware

BRUSHES, COMBS, ETC.

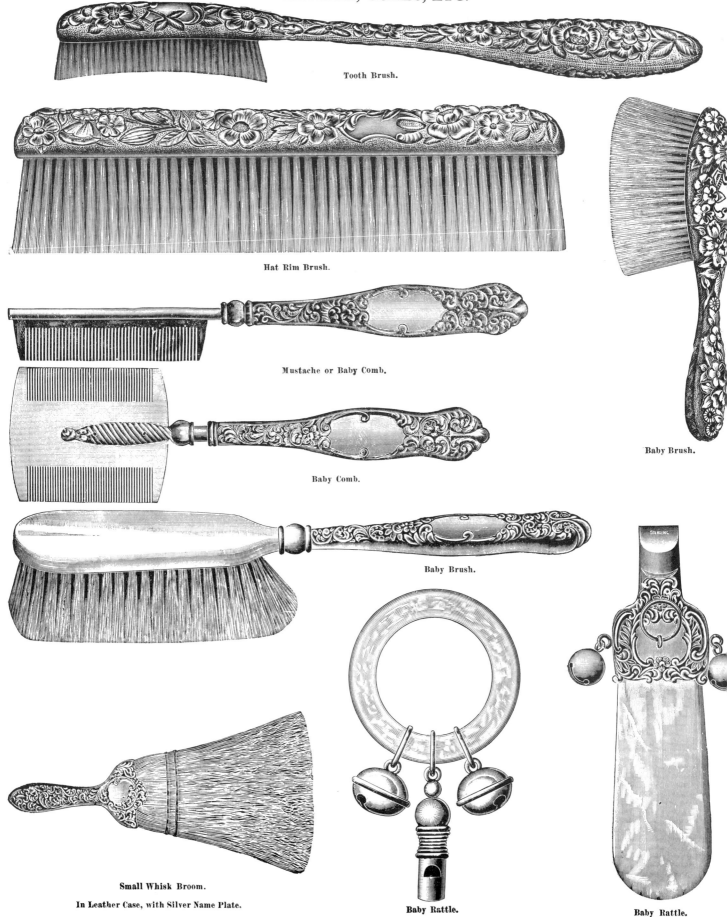

Tooth Brush.

Hat Rim Brush.

Mustache or Baby Comb.

Baby Comb.

Baby Brush.

Baby Brush.

Small Whisk Broom.

In Leather Case, with Silver Name Plate.

Baby Rattle.

Baby Rattle.

PUFF BOXES, SHOE BUTTONERS, HORN, ETC.

Shoe Buttoner.

Shoe Buttoner.

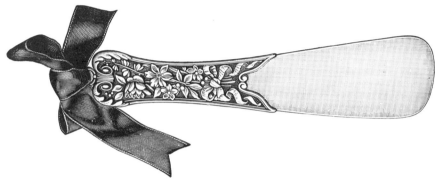

Shoe Horn.

Puff Box.

Curling Set.

Puff Box.

Patent Puff Box.

Puff Box.

Puff Box.

Puff Box.

Fine Silver Plated Hollow Ware

MANICURE SETS

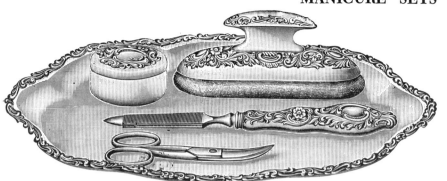

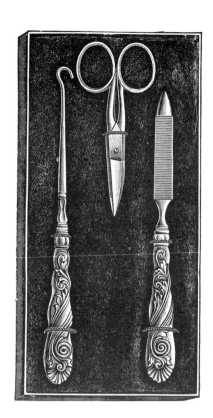

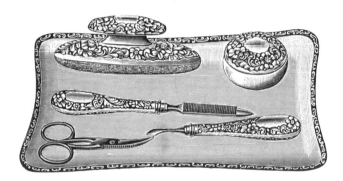

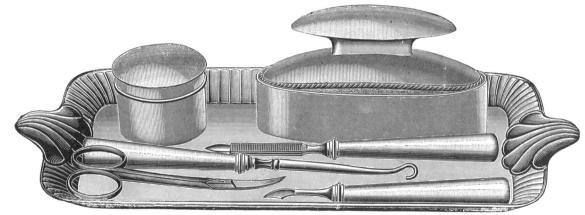

Mustache or Pocket Comb.

MANICURE AND TOILET SETS, ETC.

Pocket Comb.

Bang or Mustache Pocket Comb.

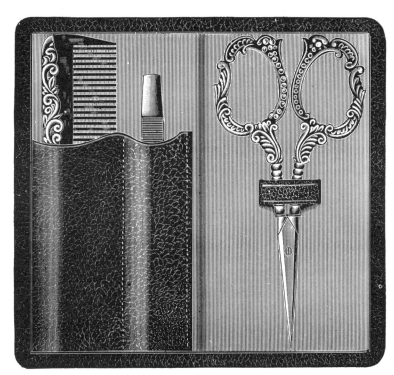

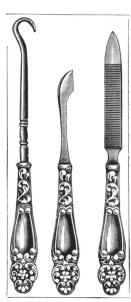

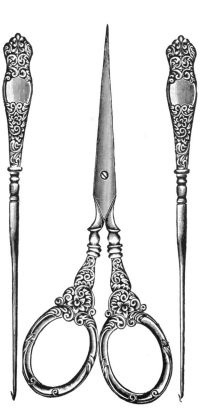

Solid Silver Novelties

PURSES, SCISSORS, ETC.

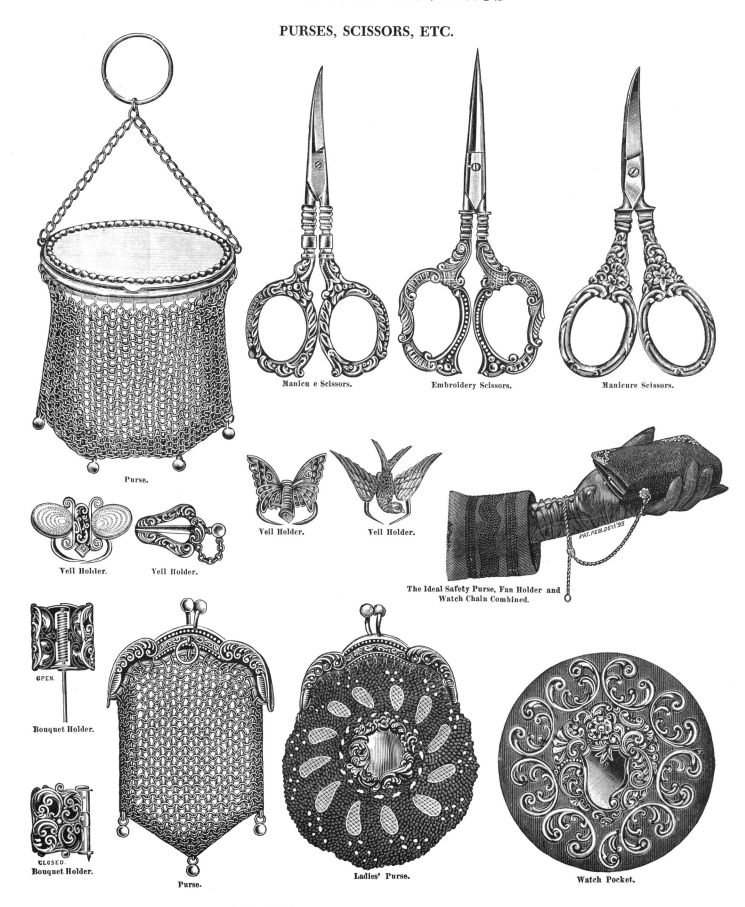

Purse.

Manicu e Scissors.

Embroidery Scissors.

Manicure Scissors.

Veil Holder.

Veil Holder.

Veil Holder.

Veil Holder.

PAT. FEB. 26th '95

The Ideal Safety Purse, Fan Holder and
Watch Chain Combined.

OPEN.

Bouquet Holder.

CLOSED.

Bouquet Holder.

Purse.

Ladies' Purse.

Watch Pocket.

LEATHER GOODS, WALLETS, ETC.

Pocket Book.

Pocket Book.

Pocket Book.

Pocket Book.

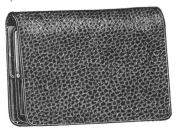

Pocket Book.

Pocket Book.

Pocket Book.

Card Case.

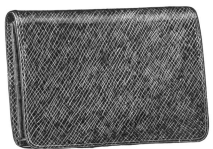

Card Case.

Pocket Book.

Poker Set.

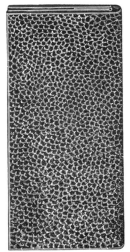

Cents' Wallet.

Writing Desk Pad.

Writing Tablet.

Gold, Silver and Rolled Gold Plate Novelties

SCARF HOLDERS, HAT BANDS, KEY RINGS, ETC.

Scarf Holder, Solid Gold, Roman.

Scarf Holder, Solid Gold, Roman.

Scarf Holder, Sterling Silver, Satin, Engraved.

Scarf Holder, Sterling Silver, Dresden Enamelled Pierced.

Scarf Holder, Sterling Silver, Dresden Enamelled.

Scarf Holder, Sterling Silver. Satin, Chased.

Scarf Holder, Sterling Silver, Satin Chased.

Scarf Holder, Sterling Silver. Dresden Enamelled.

Scarf Holder, Sterling Silver, Satin, Chased.

Scarf Holder, Sterling Silver, Satin, Bead Edge.

Scarf Holder, Rolled Gold Plate, Roman and Polished.

Scarf Holder, Rolled Gold Plate, Roman and Polished.

Scarf Holder, Rolled Gold Plate, Roman Enamelled.

Scarf Holder, Rolled Gold Plate, Polished, Chased.

Scarf Holder, Rolled Gold Plate, Polished, Chased.

Key Ring, Sterling Silver, Chased.

Key Ring, Sterling Silver, Chased.

Hat Band, Sterling Silver, Raised Edge, Satin.

Hat Band, Sterling Silver, Raised Edge.

Hat Band, Sterling Silver, Satin, Raised Edge.

Hat Band, Sterling Silver, Raised Edge, Satin.

Name Plate, Sterling Silver, for Cane or Umbrella.

Key Tag, Sterling Silver, Chased,

Coat Hanger, with Name Plate, Sterling Silver, Satin, Chased Edge.

Hat Band, Sterling Silver, Satin, Bead Edge.

Coat Hanger, with Name Plate, Sterling Silver, Bead Edge.

Coat Hanger, with Name Plate, Sterling Silver, Satin, Raised Edge.

Key Tag, for Bunch of Keys, Sterling Silver, Raised Edge, Satin, Bright Cut.

Umbrella Band, to be Sewed on Umbrella, Sterling Silver, Raised Edge, Elastic Band.

Segar Cutter Charm, Sterling Silver, Chased, Steel Blade,

Key Ring, Sterling Silver, Spring Lock.

Bicycle Tag, Sterling Silver, Satin, Bead Edge.

Bicycle Tag, Sterling Silver, Satin, Chased.

KEY CHAINS, BAG TAGS, ETC.

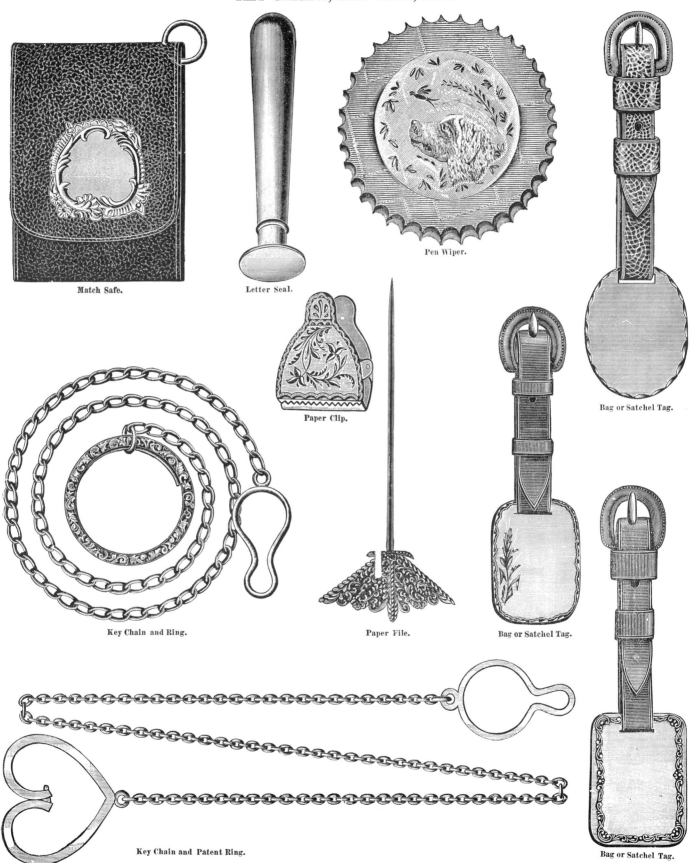

Match Safe.

Letter Seal.

Pen Wiper.

Paper Clip.

Bag or Satchel Tag.

Key Chain and Ring.

Paper File.

Bag or Satchel Tag.

Key Chain and Patent Ring.

Bag or Satchel Tag.

Fine Silver Plated Hollow Ware

ATOMIZERS

Atomizer.

Atomizer.

Atomizer.

Atomizer.

Atomizer.

Atomizer.

Atomizer.

TOILET BOTTLES, ATOMIZERS, ETC.

Nail Polisher.

Nail Polisher.

Toilet Bottle.

Toilet Bottle.

Atomizer.

Atomizer.

Flask.

Flask.

Toilet Bottle.

Ring Stand.

Fine Silver Plated Hollow Ware

INK STANDS

Ink Stand.

Ink Stand.

Ink Stand.

Ink Stand.

Ink Stand.

Ink Stand.

Ink Stand.

Ink Stand.

Ink Stand.

Ink Stand.

Ink Stand.

Fruit Knife with Nut Pick.

Vinaigrette or Salts Bottle.

Vinaigrette or Salts Bottle.

Vinaigrette or Salts Bottle.

Fruit Knife with Nut Pick.

Vinaigrette or Salts Bottle.

Razor.

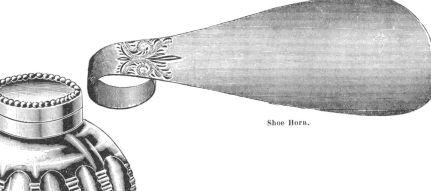

Shoe Horn.

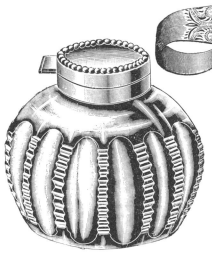

APRIL.

M	T	W	T	F	S
.	.	1	2	3	4	5
6	7	8	9	10	11	12
13	14	15	16	17	18	19
20	21	22	23	24	25	26
27	28	29	30	31	.	.

COPYRIGHTED 18

Perpetual Calendar.

Ink Stand.

Tooth Brush Bottle.

Tea Ball Holder.

Candle Stick.

Real Shell Hair Pins and Combs

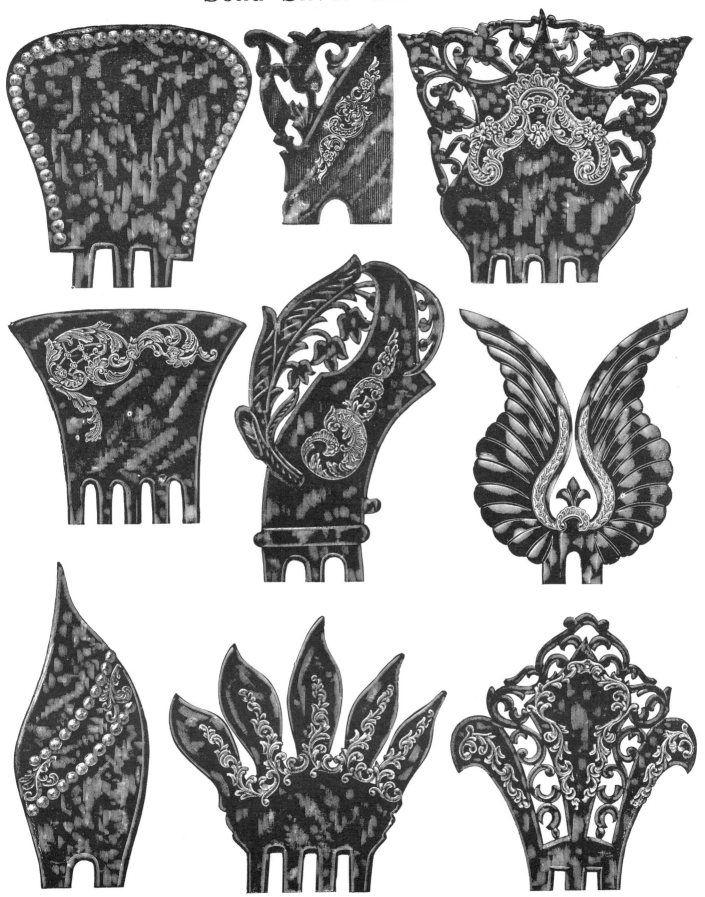

Solid Gold and Shell Hair Pins

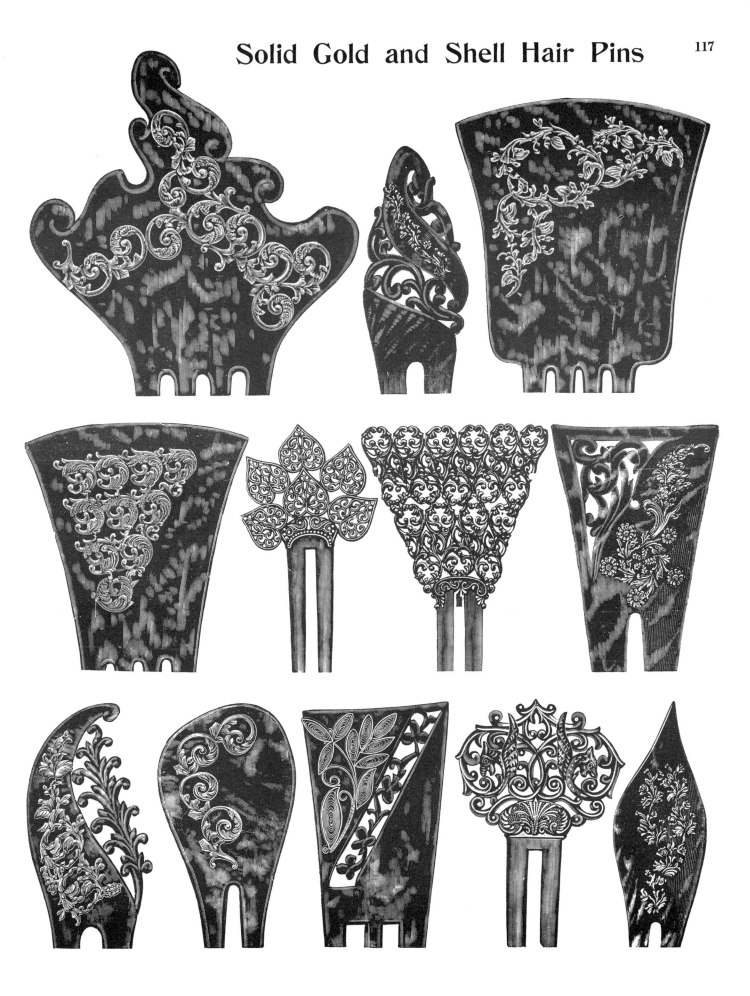

Solid Silver Hair Pins
REAL AND IMITATION TORTOISE SHELL

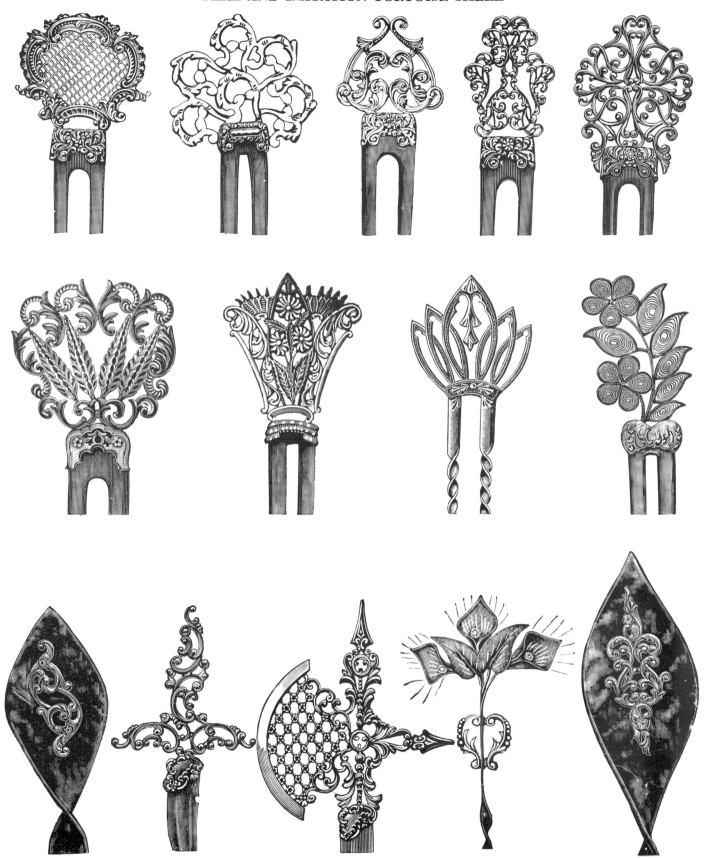

"ART" AND "COMMERCE."

"MERCURY."

"DURET." Bronze Base.

Fine Bronze Clocks

"PIZARRO" AND "CORTEZ."

"CUPID."

"VICTORY."

"CRUSADER."

ROMAN MATRON.

STAG.

HUNTER.

ZENOBIA.

MARY AND HER LAMB.

COLUMBUS.

"CABELLERO."

ARTIST.

Clock and Side Bronze Ornaments

Directum.

Elk.

Alexander.

Warrior.

Don Cæsar and Don Juan.

Standard Bearer.

Bronze, Black and Oak Enameled Iron Clocks
REAL BRONZE AND HARD BLACK JAPANNED

"SAVOY."

"CALAIS."

"ACME."

CANDELABRA.

"MAJESTIC."

CANDELABRA.

Enameled and Marbleized Mantel Clocks

HARD BLACK JAPANNED (IMITATION MARBLE)

"CARMEN."

"ELECTRA."

"CLYTIE."

"DOLPHIN."

"SYMPHONY."

"GALATEA."

Enameled and Marbleized Mantel Clocks
HARD BLACK JAPANNED (IMITATION MARBLE)

"OLYMPUS."

"REVERIE."

"COLUMBUS."

"DIADEM"

"ALCAZAR."

"FOCUS."

"LA FRANCE," WITH URN.

"SICILY."

"LA DUCHESS."

"ROSALIND."

"OXFORD."

Antique Oak Cabinet Clocks

Antique Oak Cabinet Clocks

"INGOT." Walnut.

"BULLION." Walnut. Gilt Trimmings.

"RONDO." Walnut.

"ANTLER." Oak. Walnut Trimmings.

"WASHINGTON." Oak.

"CHICAGO." Oak.

"NEW YORK." Walnut.

"BOSTON." Oak. Walnut Trimmings.

Antique Oak Cabinet Clocks

"VERONA." Polished Oak.

"BAZAR." Oak or Walnut.

Fine Regulators

BLACK WALNUT, OAK OR MAHOGANY CASES

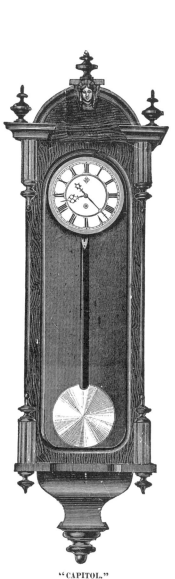

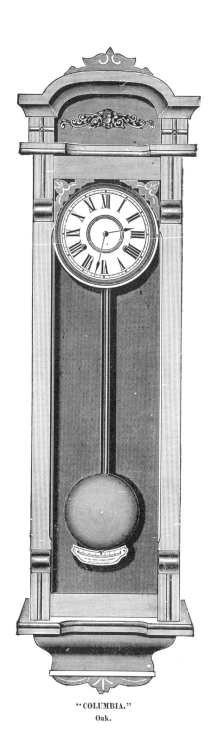

"CAPITOL."
Black Walnut, Ash, Mahogany or Oak.

"COLUMBIA."
Oak.

"PROMPT."
Black Walnut, Ash, Mahogany or Oak.

Hanging Office Clocks

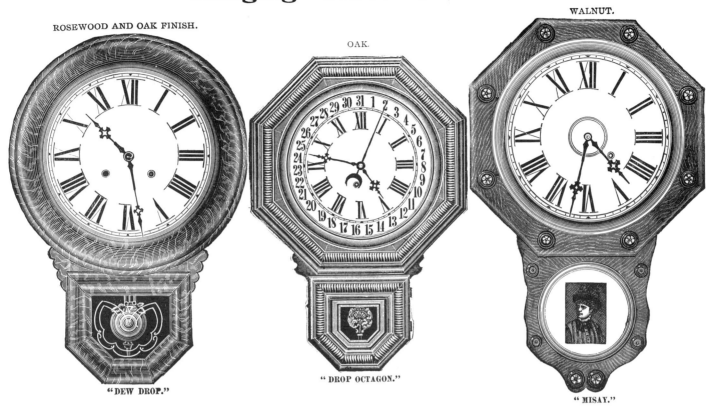

ROSEWOOD AND OAK FINISH.

"DEW DROP."

OAK.

"DROP OCTAGON."

WALNUT.

"MISAY."

ROSEWOOD.

"REFLECTOR."

OAK.

"DROP OCTAGON."

ROSEWOOD.

"IONIC CALENDAR."

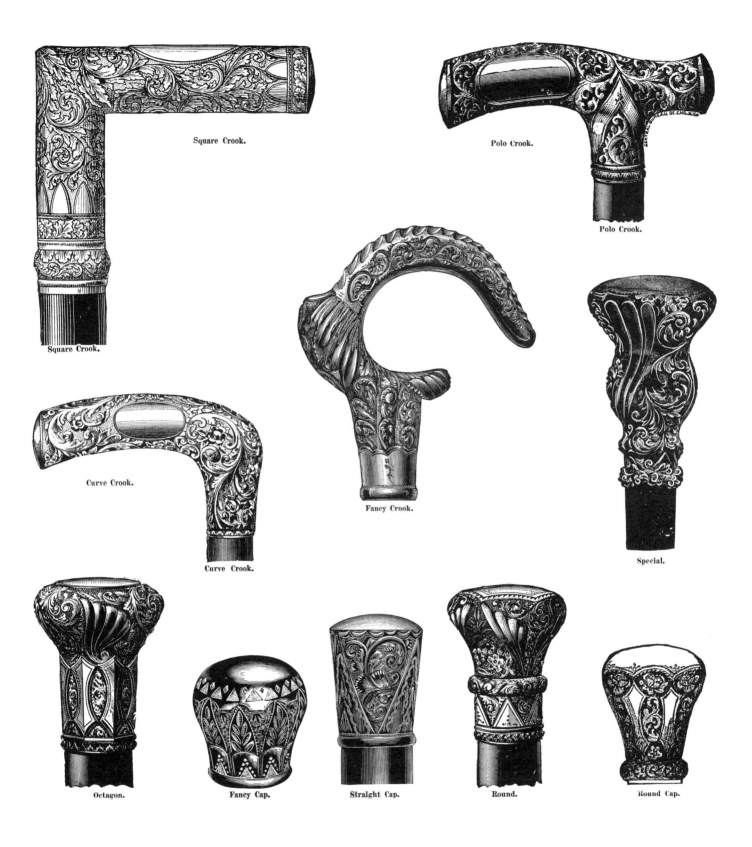

Square Crook.

Polo Crook.

Polo Crook.

Square Crook.

Curve Crook.

Fancy Crook.

Special.

Curve Crook.

Octagon.

Fancy Cap.

Straight Cap.

Round.

Round Cap.

Fine Rolled Gold Plate Headed Walking Canes

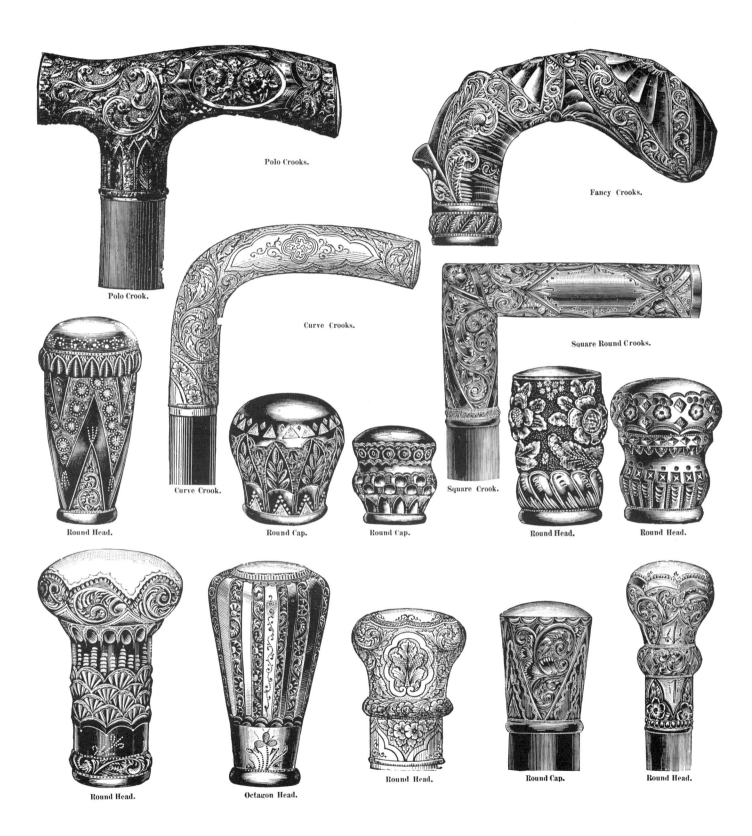

Polo Crooks.

Fancy Crooks.

Polo Crook.

Curve Crooks.

Square Round Crooks.

Curve Crook.

Square Crook.

Round Head.

Round Cap.

Round Cap.

Round Head.

Round Head.

Round Head.

Octagon Head.

Round Head.

Round Cap.

Round Head.

Fine Silk Umbrellas

ROLLED GOLD PLATE HEADS

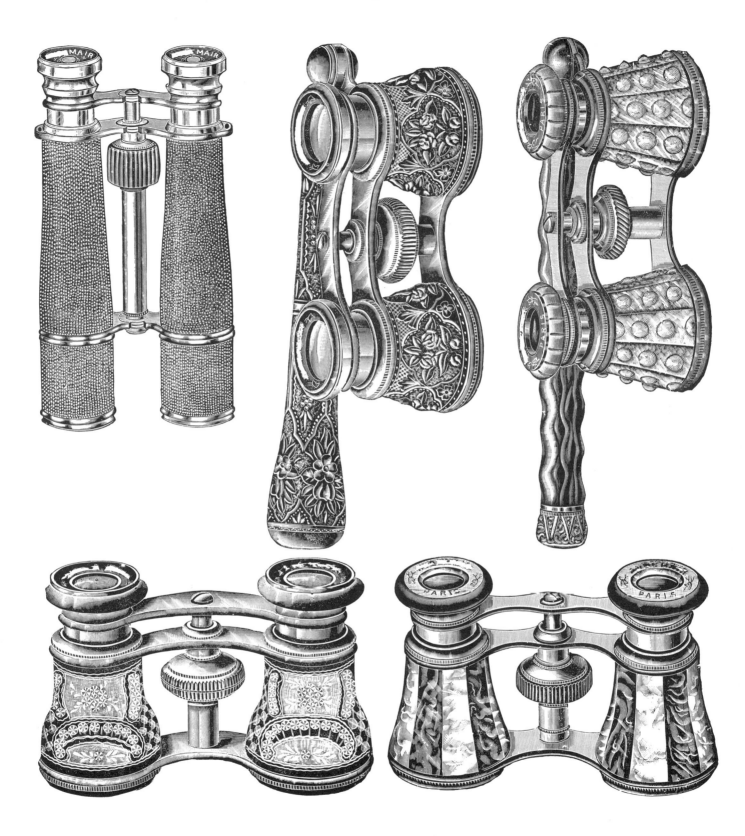

Silver Hand Chased Body.

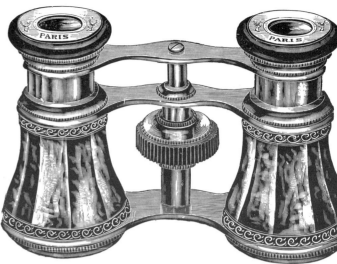

Oriental Pearl Body. Gilt Slides.

Gold Hand Chased Body

Kid Body, Nickel Slides

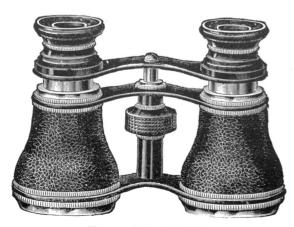

Morocco Body, Gilt Slides

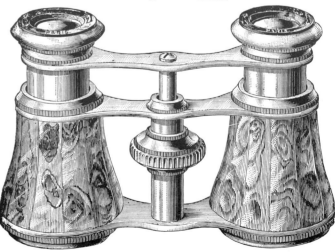

Persian Pearl Body, Gilt Slides

Day and Night Signal Glass.

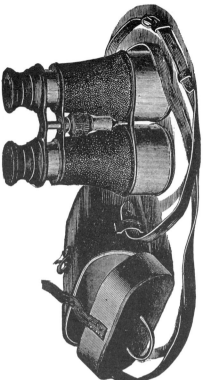

Field Glasses.

U. S. Army and Navy

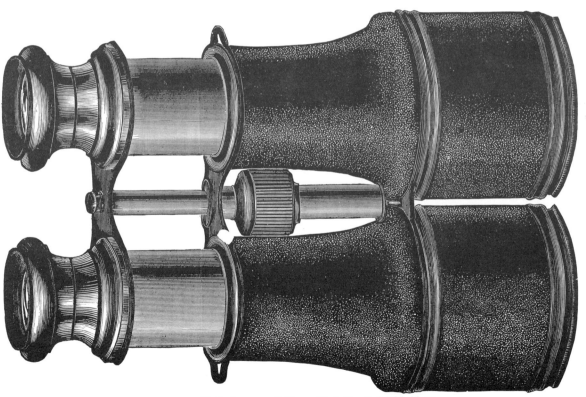

U. S. Army and Navy High Grade Field Glass.

Eye Glasses

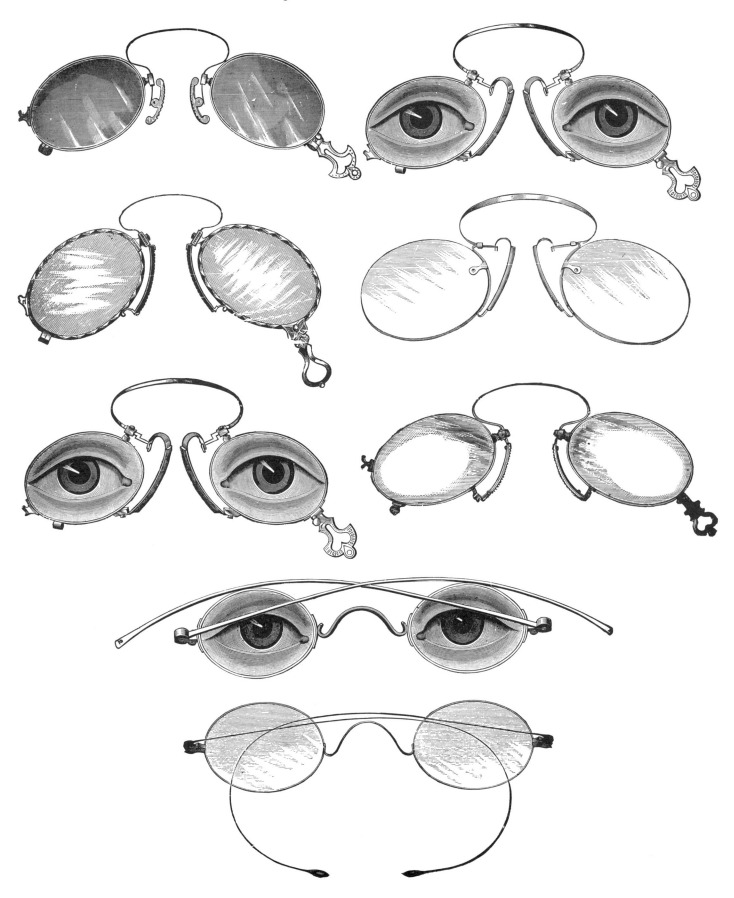

Musical Merchandise

HARMONICAS

RICHTER.

GEBRUDER LUDWIG RICHTER.

BOSS RICHTER.

GEBRUDER LUDWIG PROFESSIONAL.

EXTRA RICHTER.

GEBRUDER LUDWIG RICHTER.

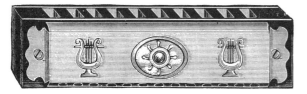

RICHTER.

GOLDEN ANCHOR.

SUPERIOR—Silver Tone.

GEBRUDER LUDWIG PATENT.

FULL CONCERT—Miniature Size.

GEBRUDER LUDWIG FULL CONCERT.

Musical Merchandise

PICCOLOS.
IN KEY OF D OR E-FLAT.

D OR E-FLAT.

D OR E-FLAT

D OR E-FLAT.

DRUMS.

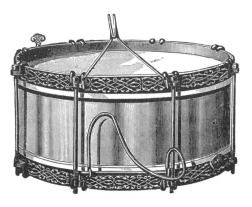

TAMBOURINE.

TAMBOURINE.

TAMBORINE.

TAMBOURINE.
Salvation Army.

Bb CORNET. BRASS.

Eb CORNET. BRASS.

Eb ALTO. BRASS.

Eb ALTO. BRASS.

Bb TENORS. BRASS.

Trombones.

German Silver, Light Action Piston Valves, Water Key.

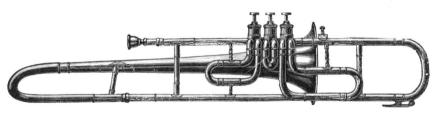

German Pump Valves, with Water Key, Music Rack and German Silver Mouth Piece.

CYMBALS. Brass.

GERMAN CONCERTINAS.

Musical Merchandise

IMPORTED ACCORDIONS

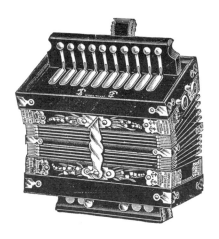 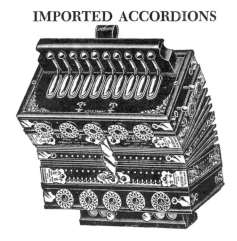 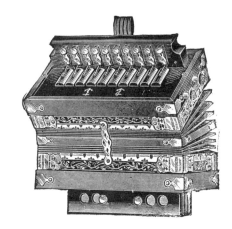

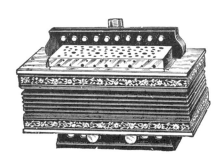  

Musical Merchandise
AMERICAN MANDOLINS

REAL OLD VIOLINS.

14 K. Solid Gold Cases

Full Shell, Engraved.

Fancy Borders and Center, Engraved.

Escalloped Center, Fancy Engraved.

Fancy Engraved, Raised Colored Gold Ornaments.

Full Engraved Escaloped Center, Raised Colored Gold Ornaments, 8 Diamonds.

Fancy Engraved, Half Filled Center, Raised Colored Gold Ornaments.

Top and Bottom Engraved.

Fancy Engraved.

Vermicelli Borders Engraved.

14 K. Solid Gold Watches

Bascine Full Engraved.

Top and Bottom Engraved.

Bascine Full Engraved

Bascine Fancy Engraved.

Vermicelli Center. Fancy Engraved.

Vermicelli Center, Landscape Engraved.

Full Shell, Engraved.

Full Fancy Engraved.

Escaloped Center, Full Engraved.

14 K. Solid Gold Cases

"DOG."   "FIRE ENGINE."   "STALLION."

"LOCOMOTIVE."   "YACHT."   "STEAMBOAT."

Gold Chronographs and Repeating Watches

Plain or Engine Turned, Split 1-5 Second Chronograph.
Antique Pendant.

Plain or Engine Turned, Repeater and Chronograph.

Plain or Engine Turned, 1-5 Second Chronograph.

Plain or Engine Turned, Split 1-5 Second Chronograph.

Engine Turned, Split 1-5 Second Chronograph.

Engine Turned Repeater, Split Second Chronograph.

Vermicelli Borders, Engraved.

Engine Turned or Engraved Case.

Vermicelli Borders, Engraved.

Gold Electro Plated Cases

Vermicelli Borders, Engraved.

Full Vermicelli, Star Engraved.

Engine Turned.

Full Engraved.

Assorted, Fancy Engraved.

Fancy Borders, Bird, Horse Head or Dog Head
Engraved.

Assorted, Fancy Engraved.

Full Vermicelli, Star Engraved.

Raised Colored Gold Ornaments, 3 Diamonds, Full
Engraved.

Escaloped Vermicelli Borders, Engraved.

10 and 14 K. Gold Filled Cases

Rolled Gold Plate Cases

Escalloped Center, Full Engraved.

Full Vermicelli, Star Engraved.

Durand Engraved.

Fancy Borders, Engraved.

Full Vermicelli Engraved.

Escaloped Vermicelli Border and Center
Engraved.

Vermicelli Center Durand Engraved.

Fancy Engraved.

Escaloped Center, Fancy Engraved. Raised
Colored Gold Ornaments.

Fancy Engraved, Raised Colored Gold
Ornaments.

Fancy Engraved, Raised Colored Gold
Ornaments.

Fancy Engraved.

Engine Turned.

Fancy Borders, Engraved.

Escalloped Center, Full Engraved.

Fancy Borders, Engraved.

14 K. Solid Gold Cases

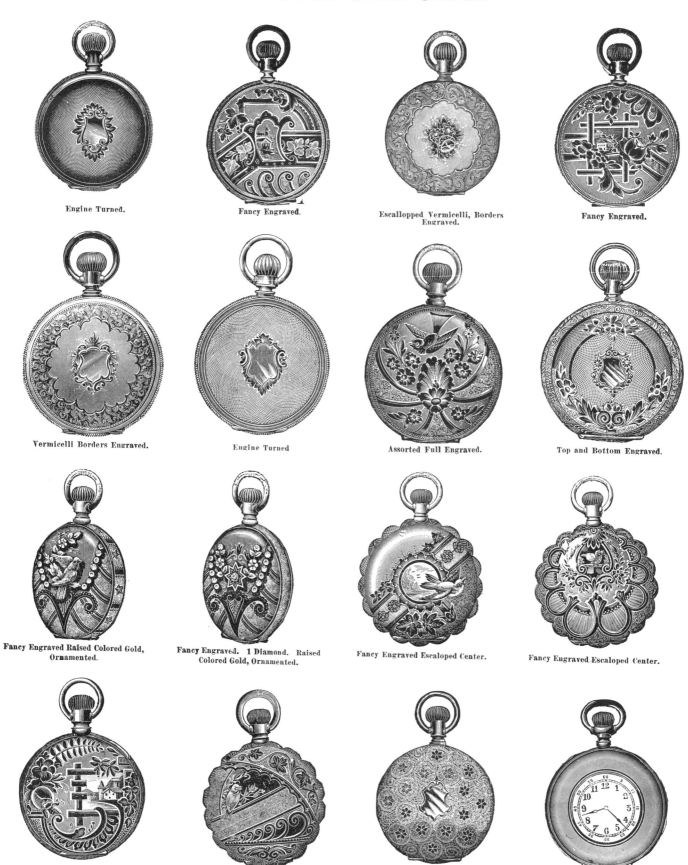

Engine Turned.

Fancy Engraved.

Escallopped Vermicelli, Borders Engraved.

Fancy Engraved.

Vermicelli Borders Engraved.

Engine Turned

Assorted Full Engraved.

Top and Bottom Engraved.

Fancy Engraved Raised Colored Gold, Ornamented.

Fancy Engraved. 1 Diamond. Raised Colored Gold, Ornamented.

Fancy Engraved Escaloped Center.

Fancy Engraved Escaloped Center.

Full Engraved.

Escaloped Center, Fancy Engraved.

Full Vermicelli Star Engraved.

Bascine Plain Polished.

14 K. Solid Gold Cases

Vermicelli Border and Center Engraved.

Fancy Engraved.

Engine Turned.

Fancy Engraved Vermicelli Center.

Assorted Fancy Engraved.

Fancy Engraved Vermicelli Center

Fancy Engraved, Escaloped Center.

Fancy Engraved, Vermicelli Center.

Full Engraved, Chased Borders and Center. Sk'tor

Chased Borders and Center, Engine Turned or Plain.

Assorted, Fancy Engraved.

Engine Turned or Plain Polish.

Fancy Engraved, Vermicelli Bezel.

Full Engraved.

Full Engraved Escaloped Center.

Fancy Engraved Escaloped Center.

Gold and Silver Watches
HUNTING AND OPEN FACE, STEM WIND AND SET

Gold. Plain Polished, Corrugated.

Gold. Plain Polished.

Gold. Plain Polished.

Gold. Assorted Engraved.

AMERICAN CHATELAINE WATCHES

Silver. 13 Ligne, Stem Wind and Set.

Silver. 10 Ligne, Stem Wind and Set.

Silver. 13 Ligne, Stem Wind and Set.

Silver. 13 Ligne, Hunting, Stem Wind and Set, Assorted, Fancy Engraved.

Fancy Full Engraved, Raised Colored Gold Ornaments.

Vermicelli Center, Raised Colored Gold Ornaments.

Plain Durand Engraved.

Fancy Engraved Vermicelli Center.

Vermicelli Borders, Plain Center, Engine Turned or Plain Backs.

Fancy Engraved Vermicelli Center.

Full Engraved.

Fancy Full Engraved.

Silk Ribbon, Lorgnette or Guard, Fob and Vest Chains

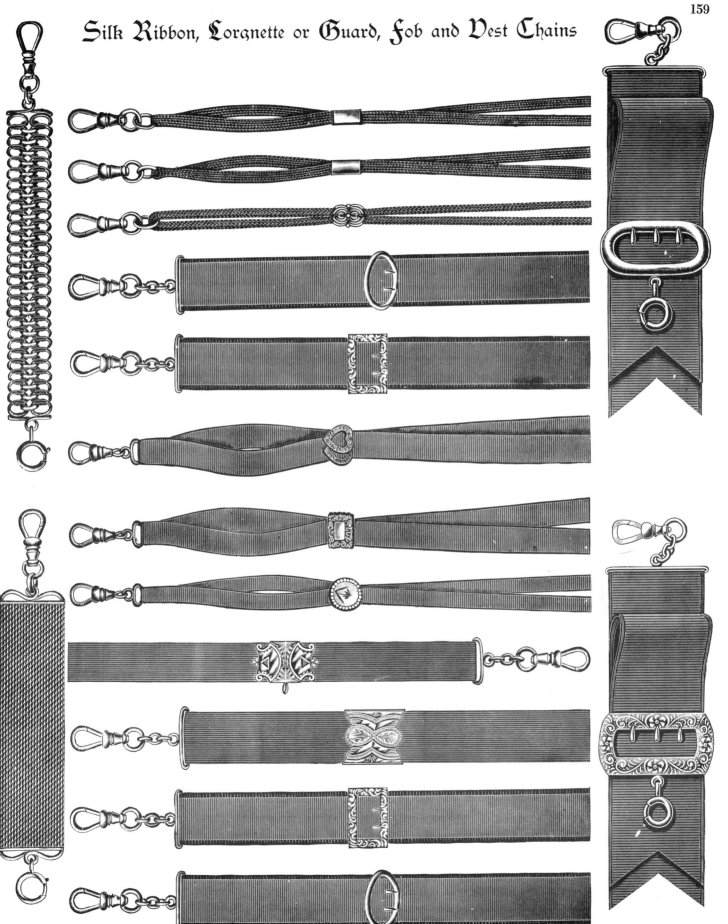

Rolled Gold Plate Vest Chains

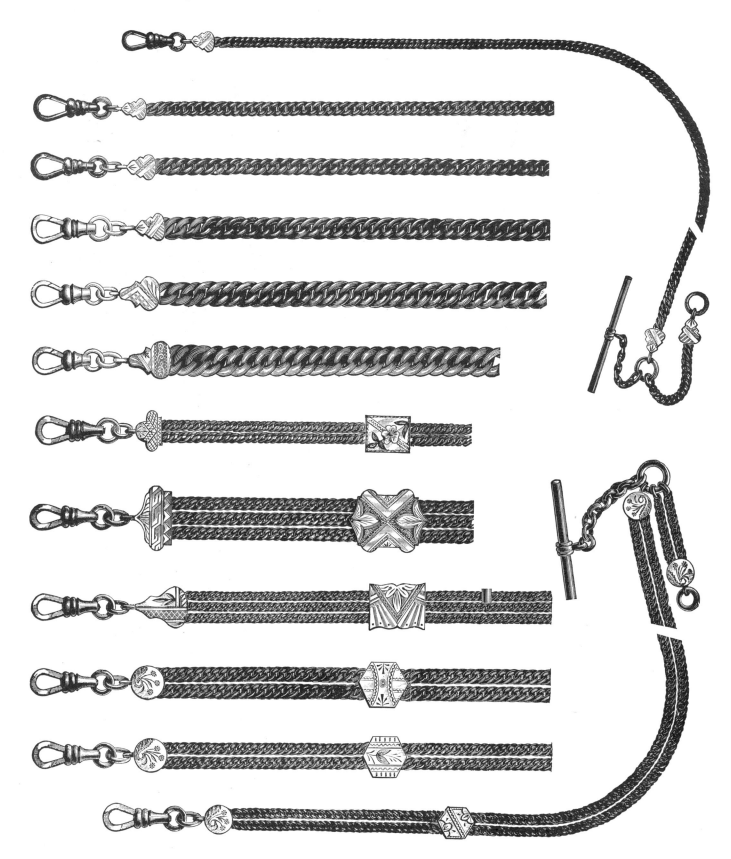

Silk Braided Vest Chains

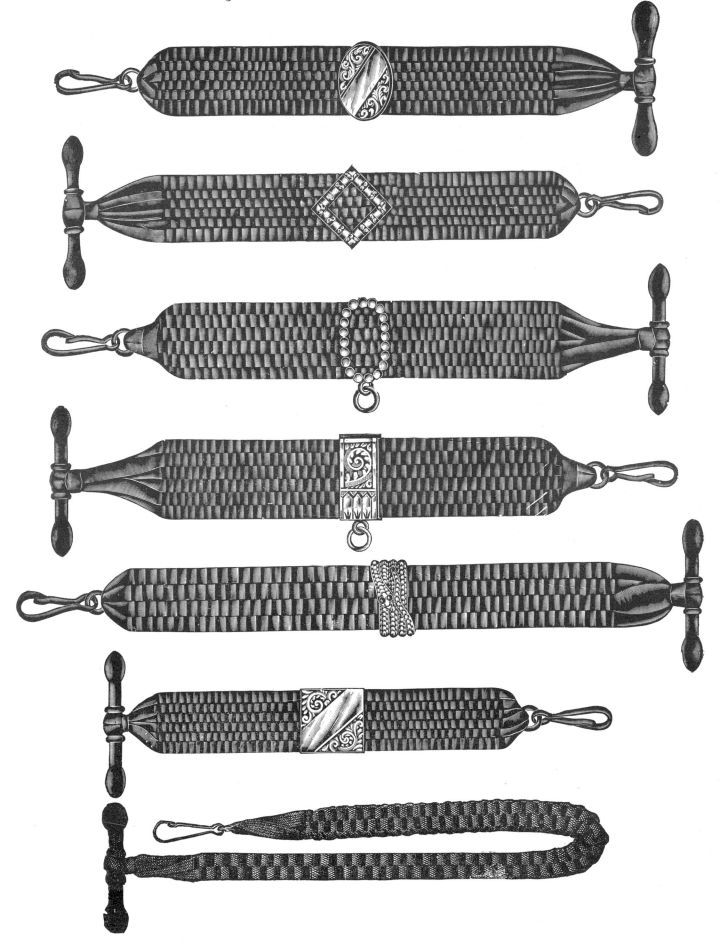

Silk Ribbon Fob Chains

Silk Ribbon Fob Chains, with Seal Charms

Solid Gold Vest Chains

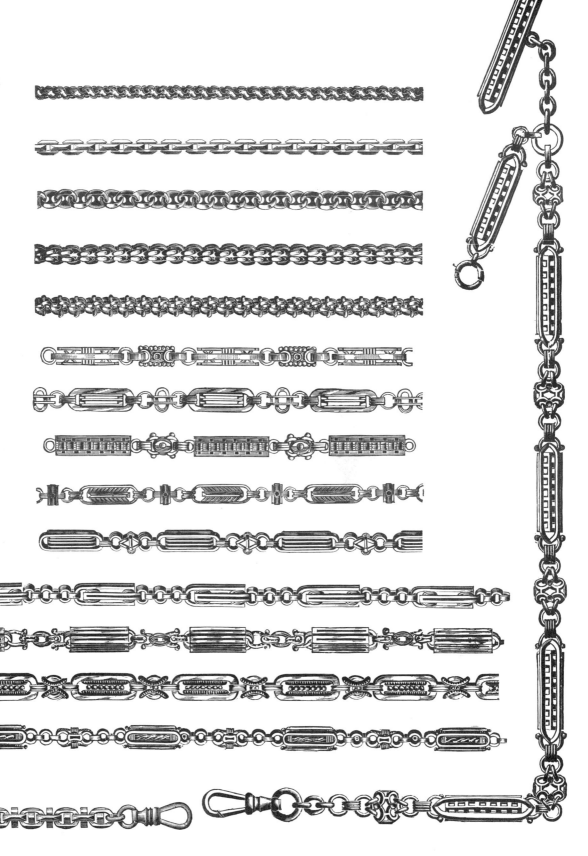

Rolled Gold Plate Vest Chains

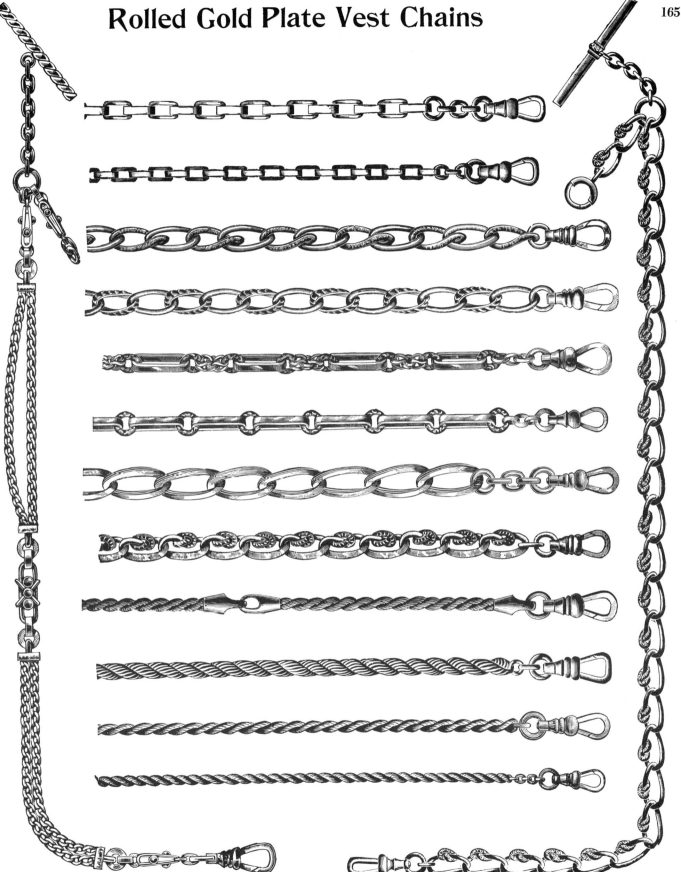

18K. Gold Filled Vest Chains

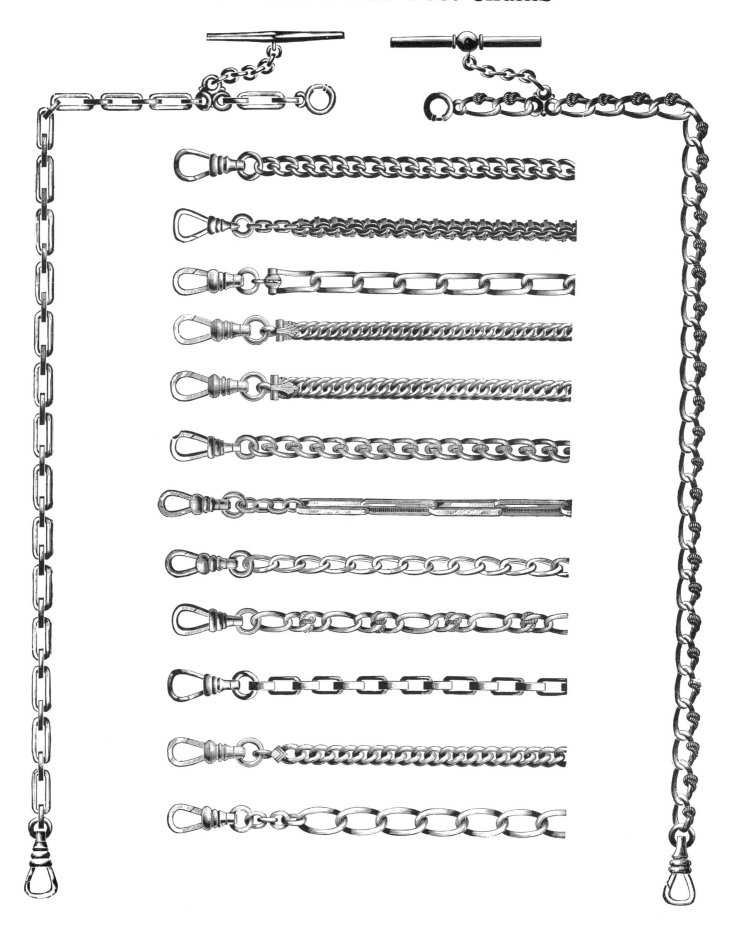

18 K. Gold Filled Vest Chains

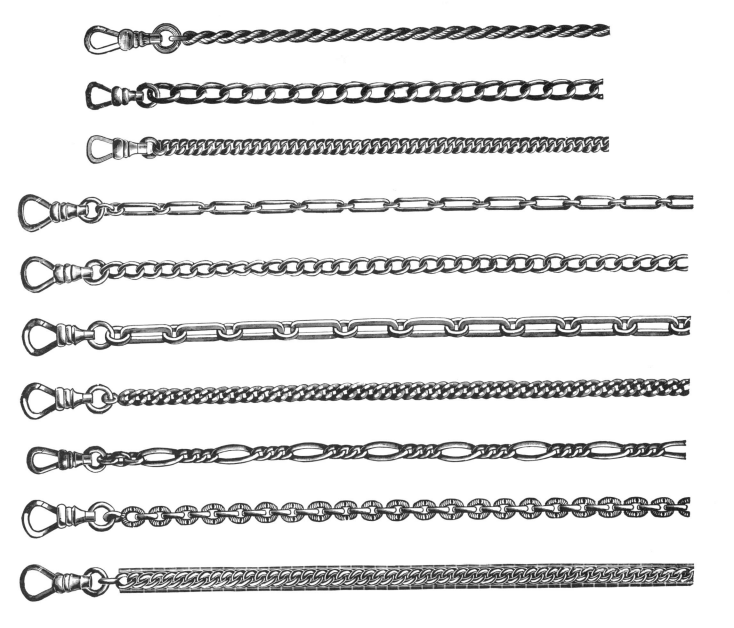

Rolled Gold Plate Vest Chains

Solid Silver Vest Chains

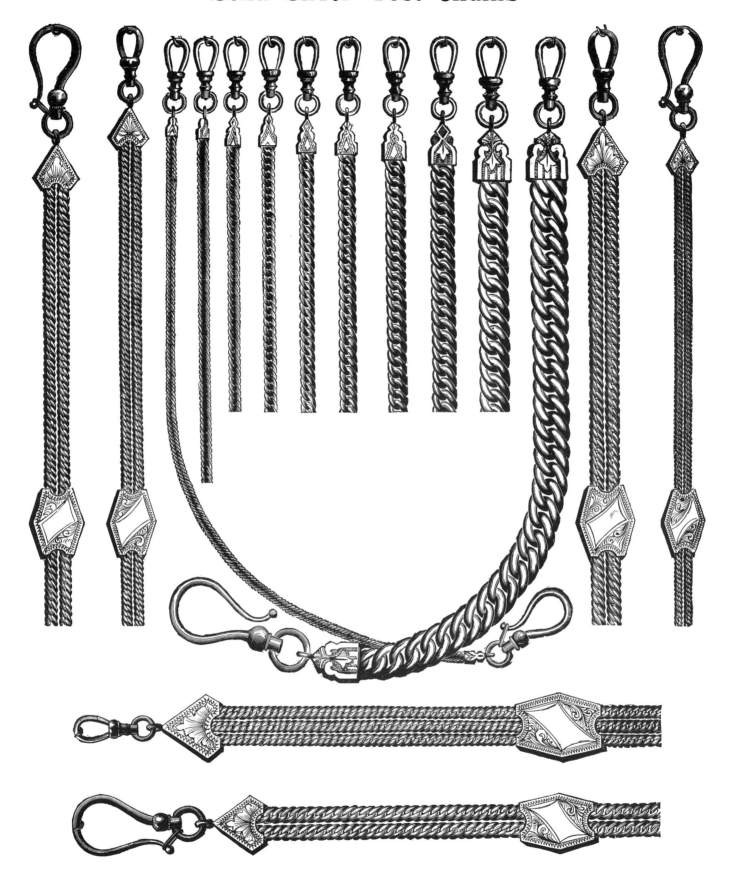

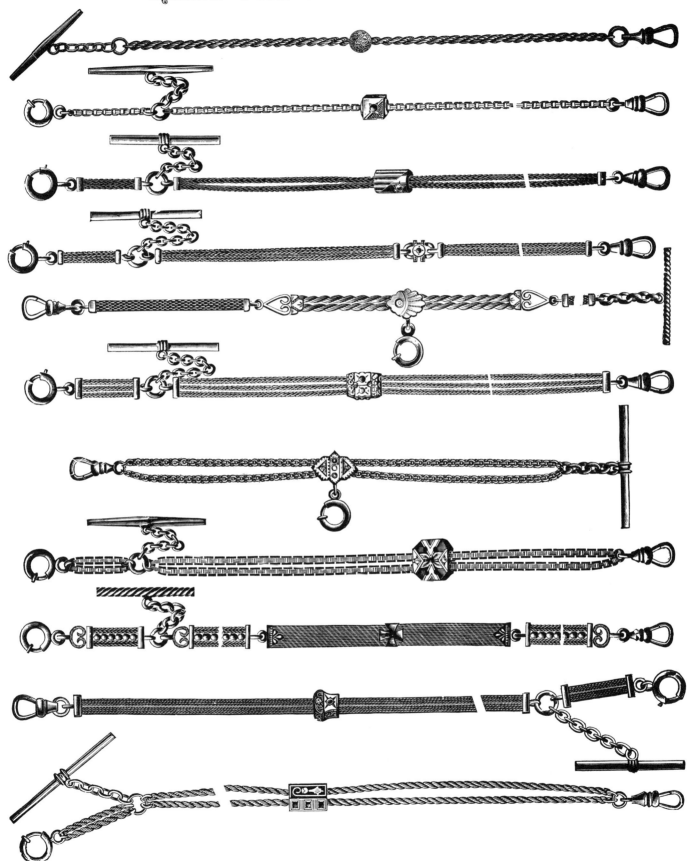

Rolled Gold Plate Vest Chains

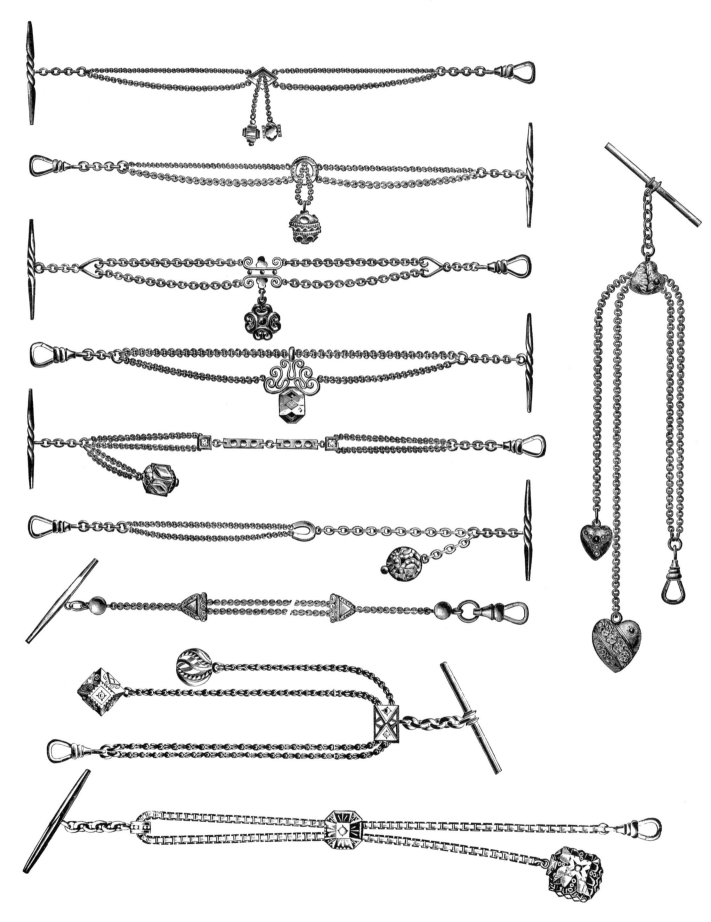

Rolled Gold Plate Victoria Chains

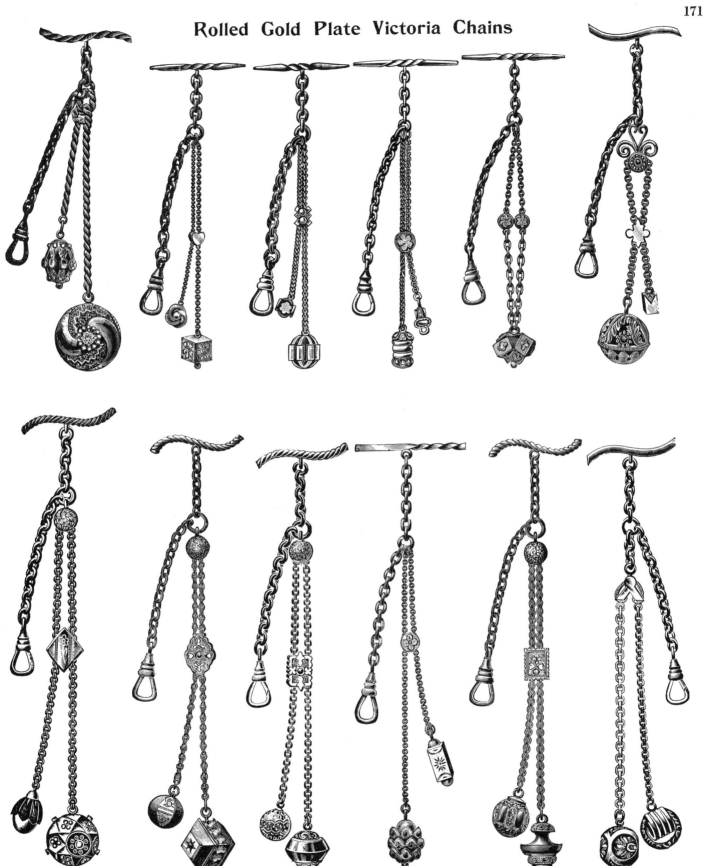

Solid Gold Victoria Chains

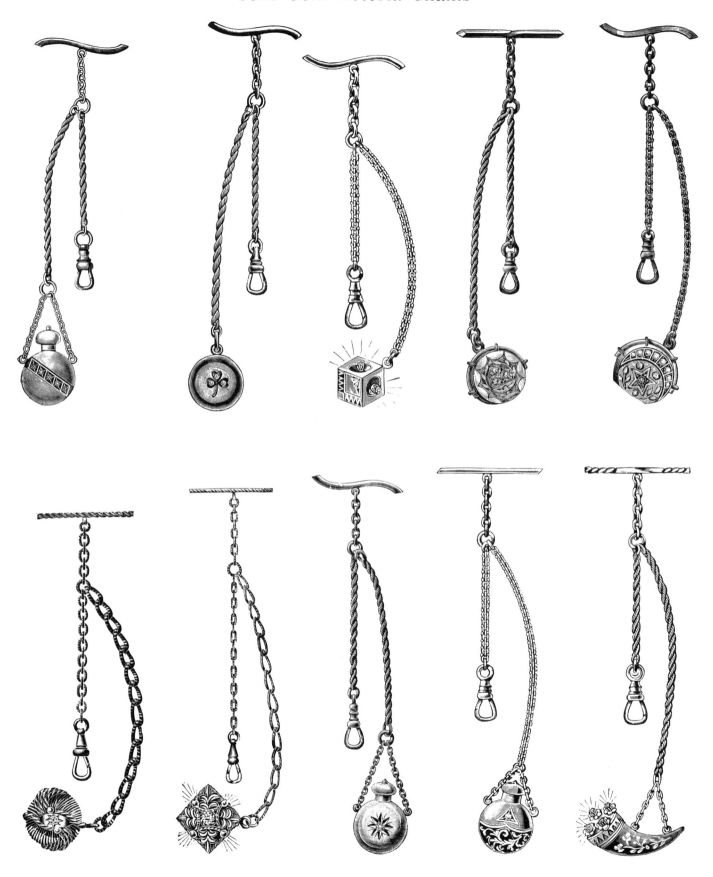

Rolled Gold Plate Victoria Chains

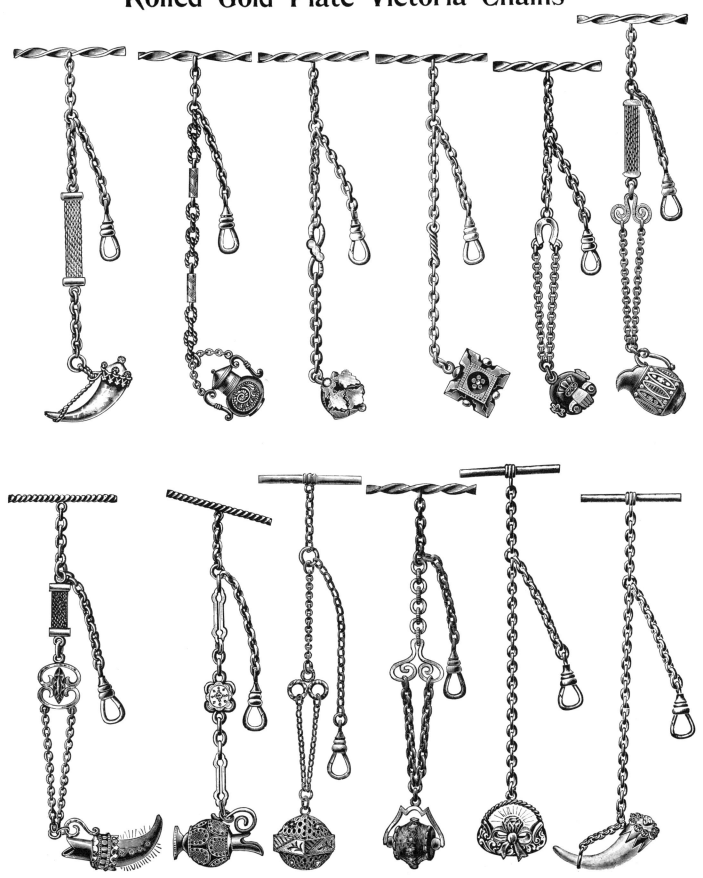

Rolled Gold Plate Victoria Chains

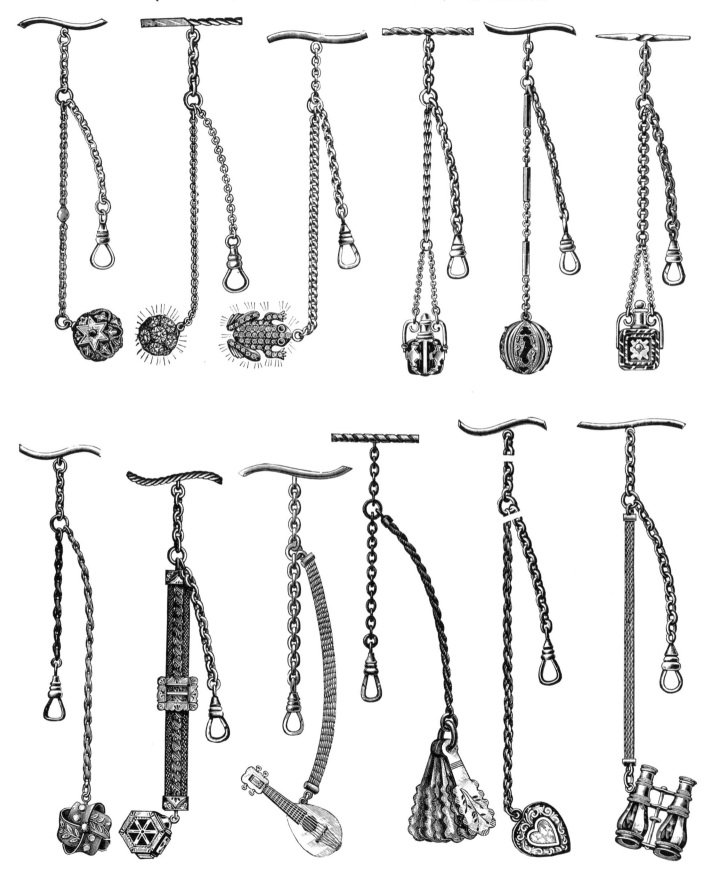

Rolled Gold Plate Victoria Chains

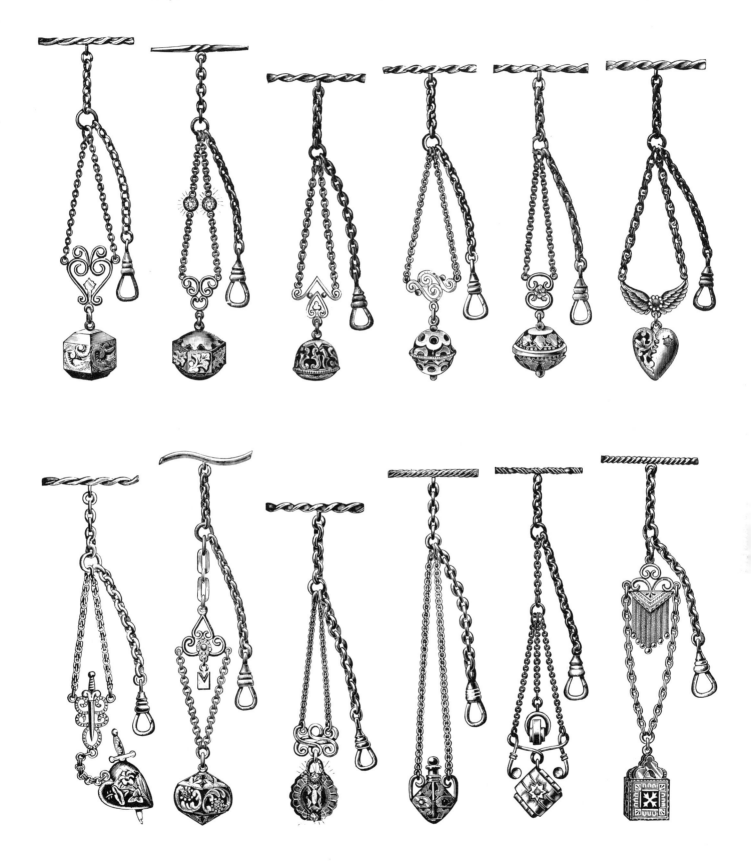

Hair Chain Mountings

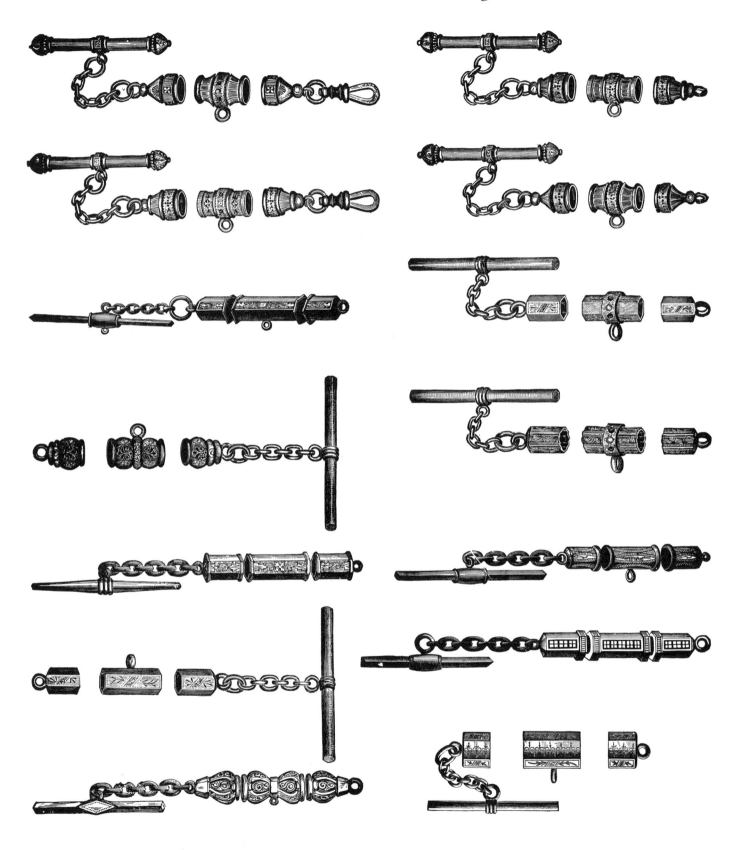

Solid Gold, Sterling Silver and Rolled Gold Plate Chatelaines and Empress Chains

Solid Silver Novelties

BRACES AND GARTERS

Gents' Garter.

Sleeve Garters.

Braces.

Braces.

Braces.

Braces.

Solid Silver Novelties
BELTS

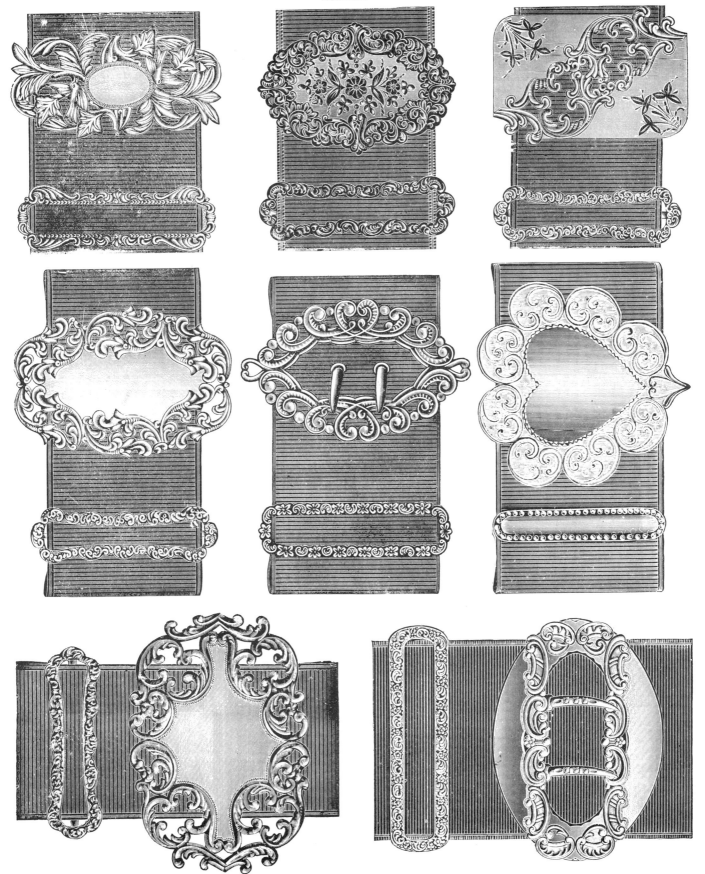

Solid Silver Novelties
FAN, TRILBY HEART AND MUFF HOLDER

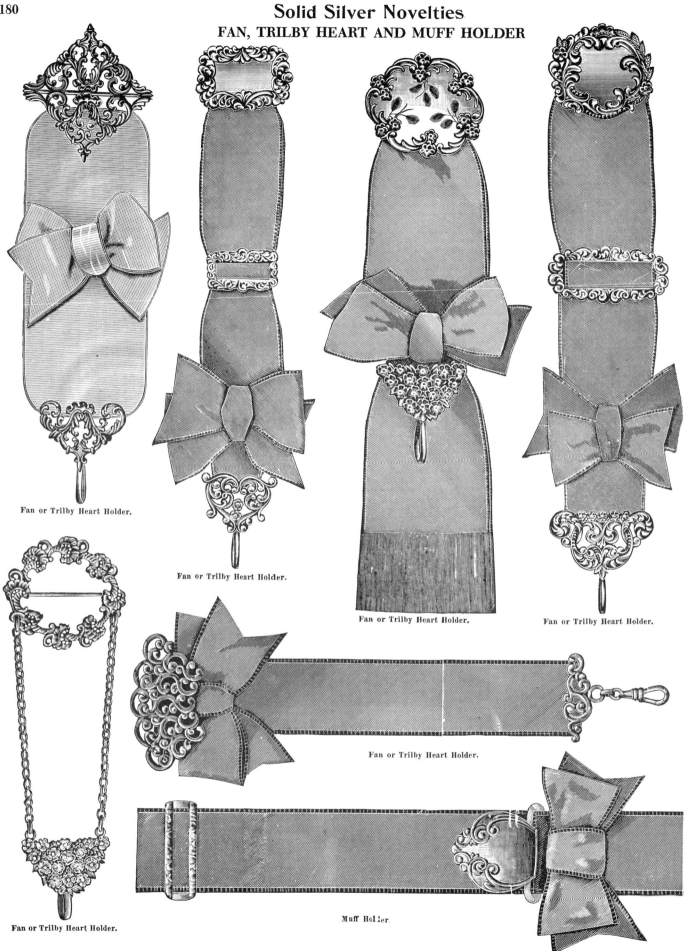

Fan or Trilby Heart Holder.

Fan or Trilby Heart Holder.

Fan or Trilby Heart Holder.

Fan or Trilby Heart Holder.

Fan or Trilby Heart Holder.

Fan or Trilby Heart Holder.

Muff Holder

GARTERS

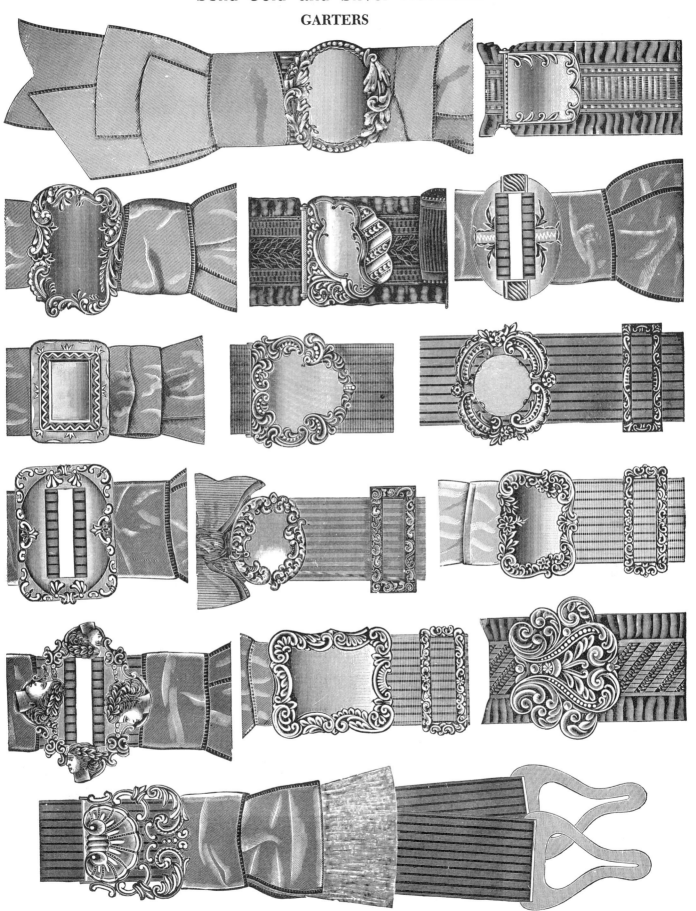

Rolled Gold Plate Locket Charms

Rolled Gold Plate Seal Charms.

Rolled Gold Plate Locket Charms

Rolled Gold Plate Charms

Solid Gold Side Lockets

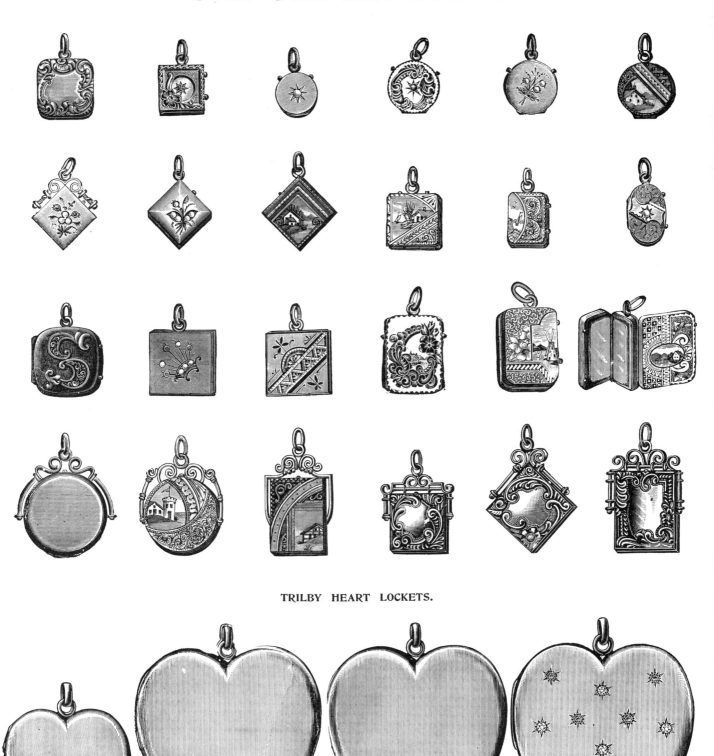

TRILBY HEART LOCKETS.

Diamond Jewelry
LOCKETS

Diamond Jewelry

LOCKETS

CUFF BUTTONS

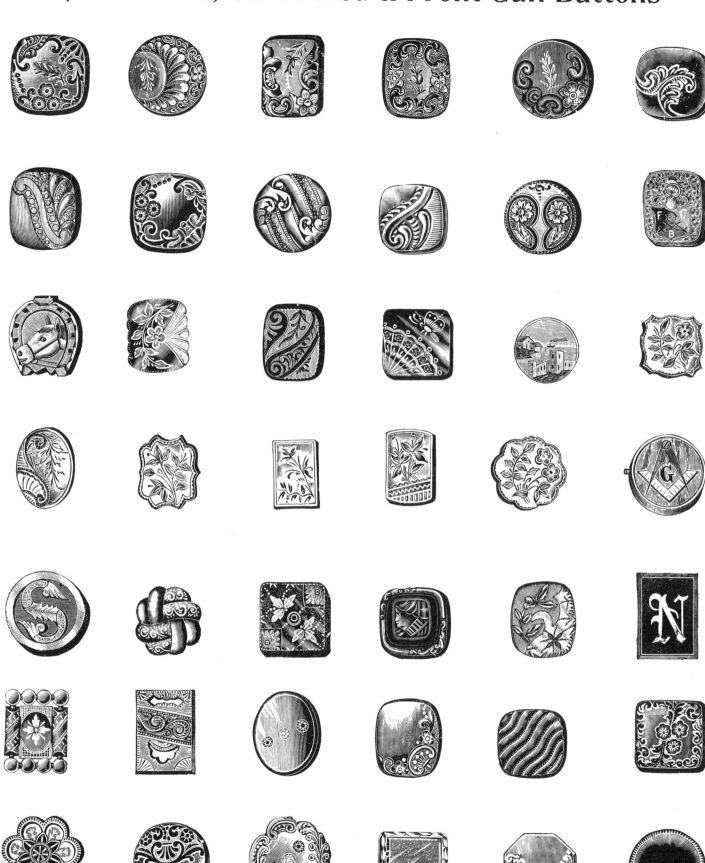

Rolled Gold Plate Cuff Buttons

Original Separable Cuff Buttons

Carved Pearl Cuff Buttons

Solid Gold Cuff Buttons

Rolled Gold Plate Cuff Buttons

Ladies' Lever Cuff Buttons

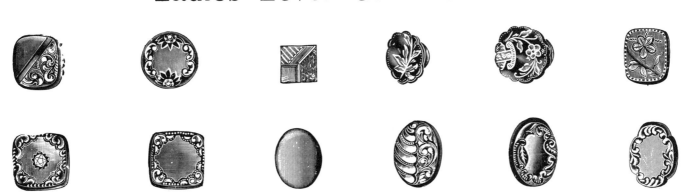

Solid Silver Cuff Buttons

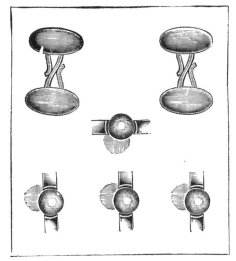
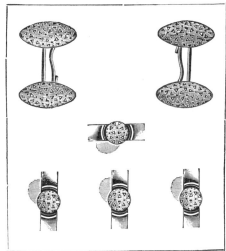
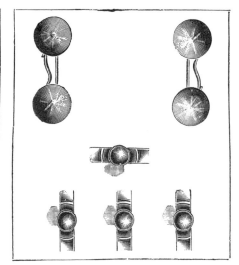
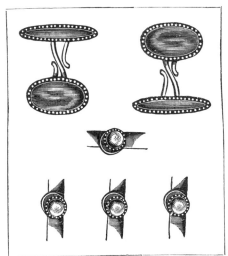

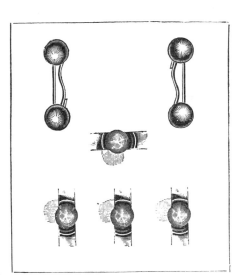
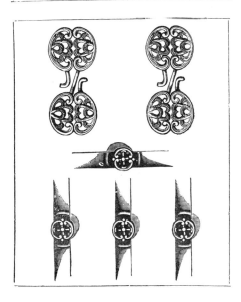
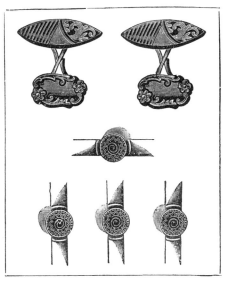

Sterling Silver Button Sets

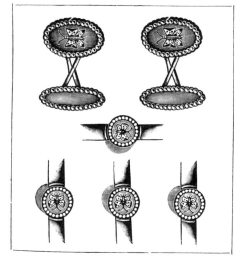

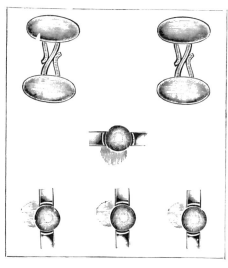
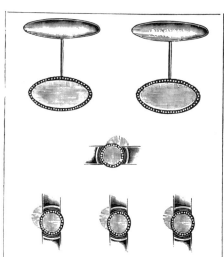
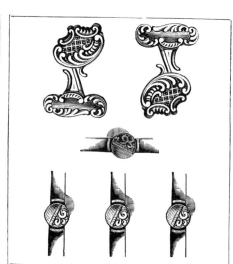
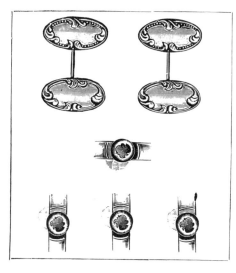
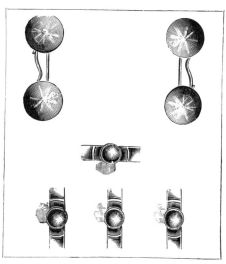
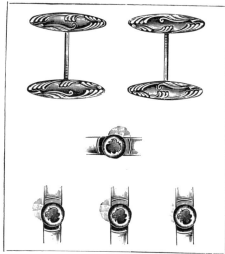

BROOCHES OR PENDANTS

Diamond Jewelry

BROOCHES OR PENDANTS

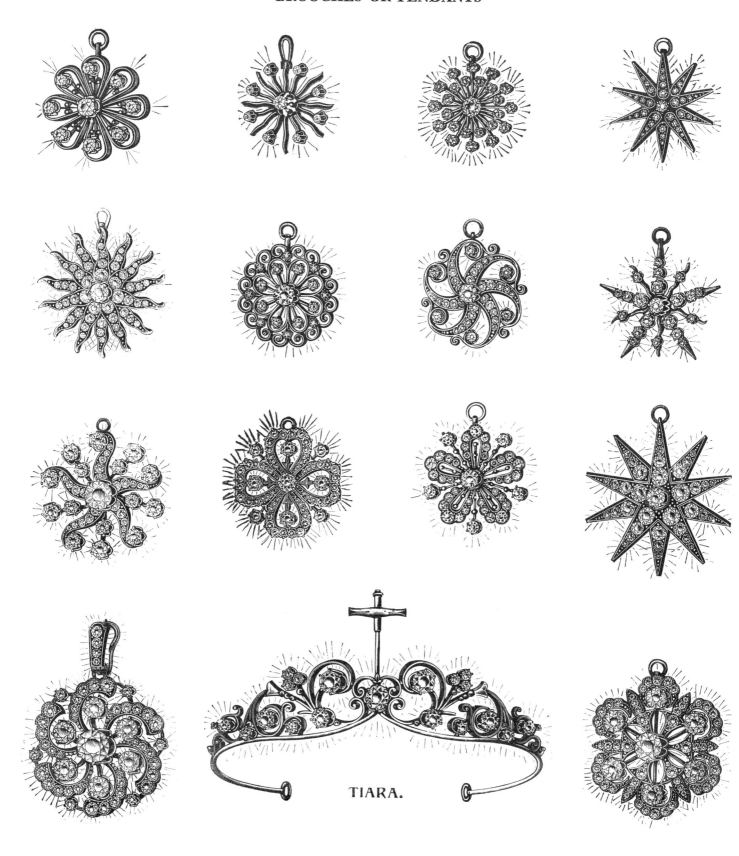

TIARA.

Diamond Jewelry

BROOCHES OR PENDANTS

Solid Gold Brooch Pins

Solid Gold Brooch Pins

Rolled Gold Plate Brooch Pins

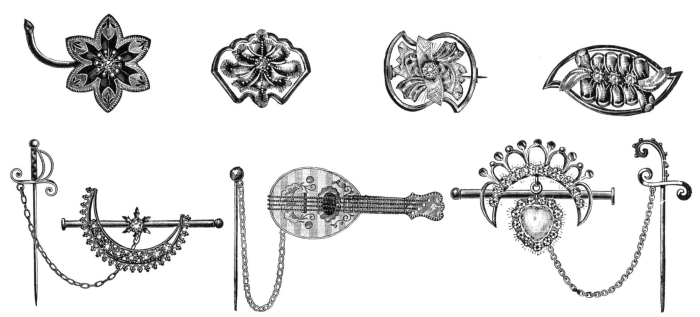

Onyx Jet and Crapestone Brooch and Lace Pins

Rolled Gold Plate Brooch Pins

Diamond Jewelry

RINGS

Fine Solid Gold Rings

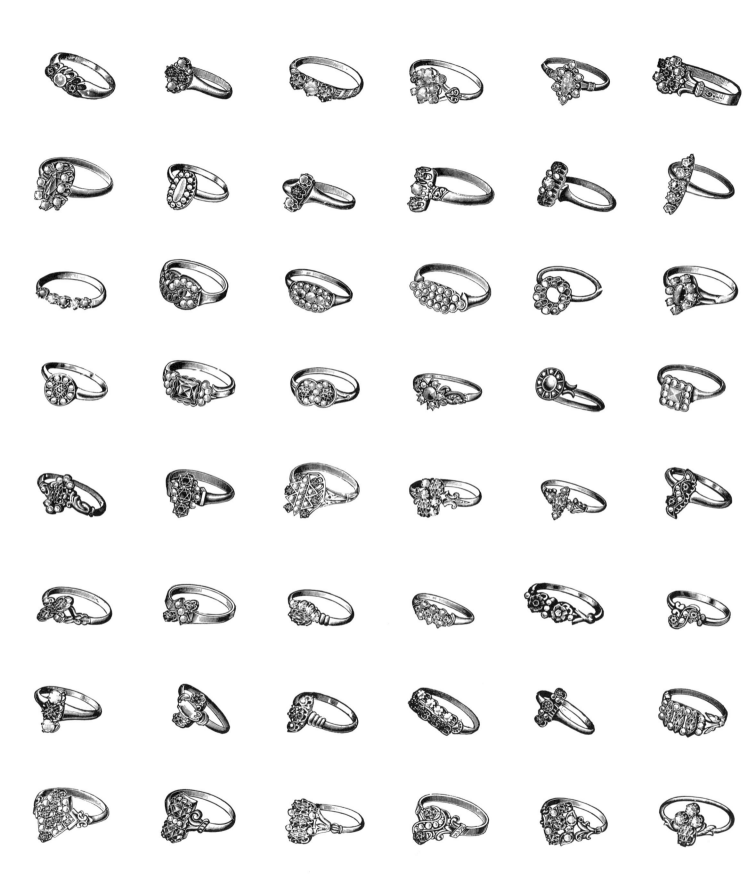

Fine Solid Gold Rings

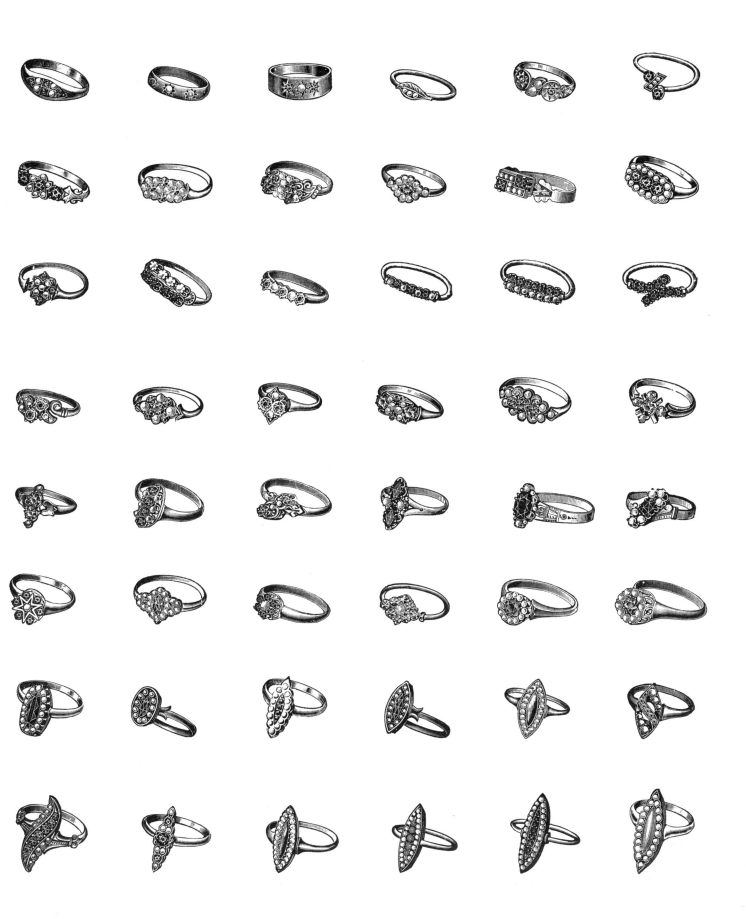

Fine Solid Gold Rings

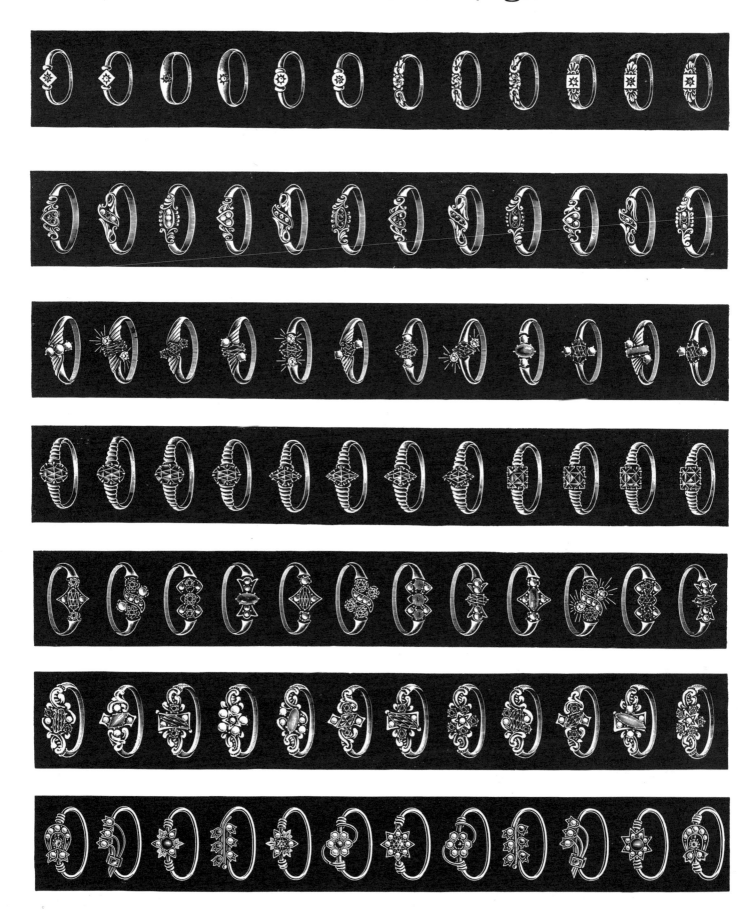

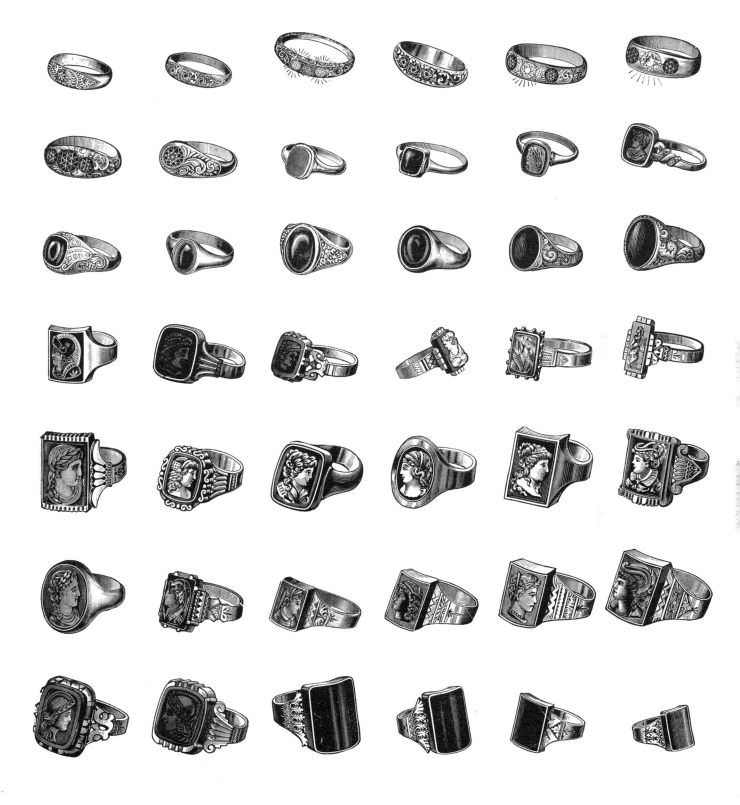

Fine Rolled Gold Plate Rings

Solid Gold Band and Emblem Rings

Rolled Gold Plate Ear Drops

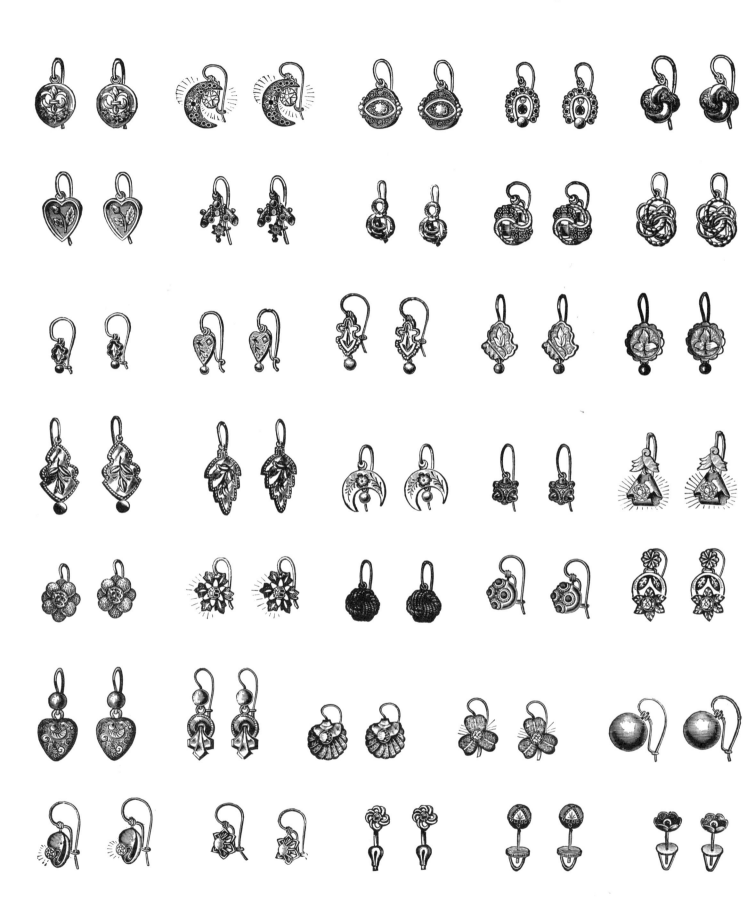

Solid Gold Ear Drops

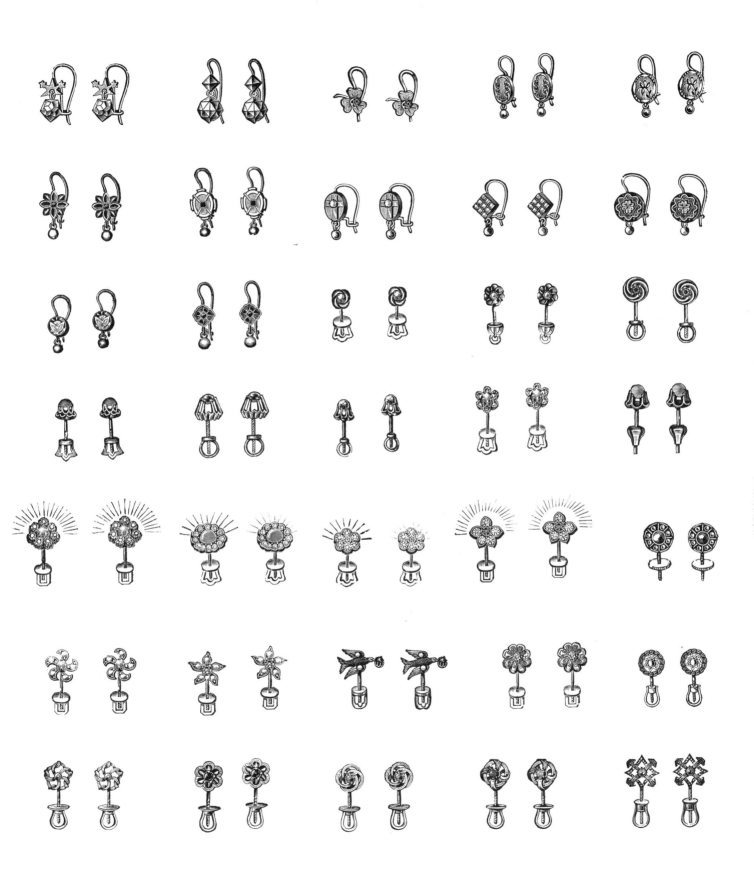

Solid Gold Ear Drops

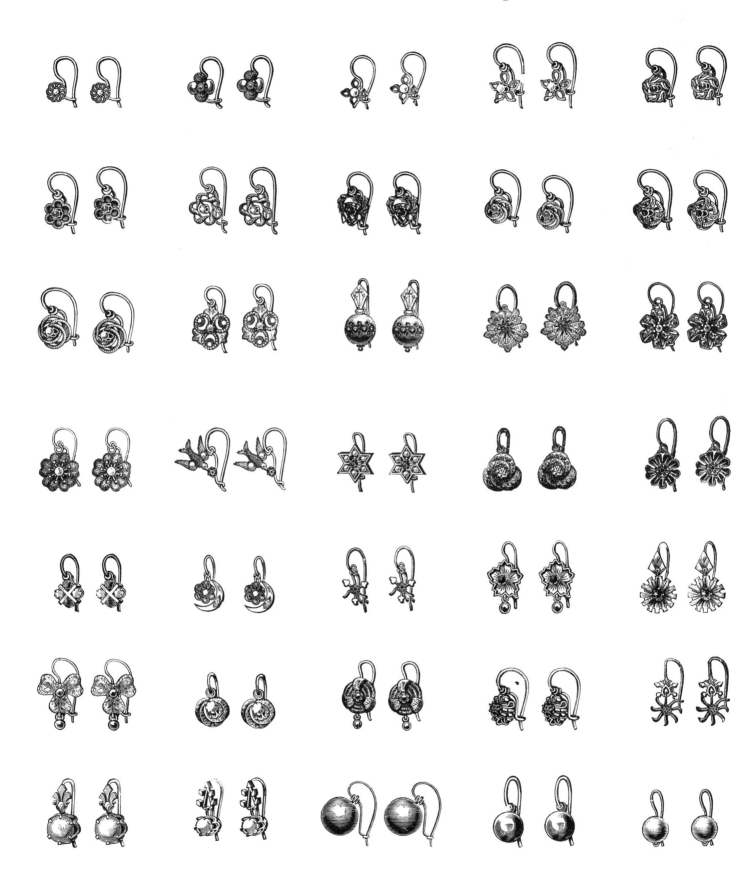

Rolled Gold Plate Studs
FINE WHITE STONE BRILLIANTS

Rolled Gold Plate Studs.

Solid Gold Bracelets

Rolled Gold Plate Bracelets

Diamond Jewelry

NECKLACES

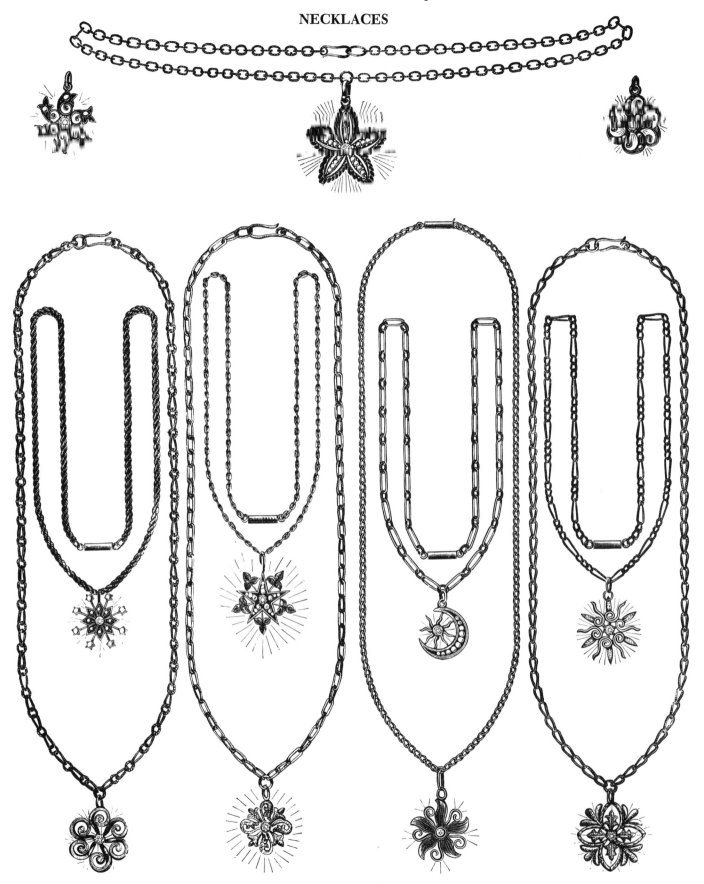

Solid Gold Necklaces

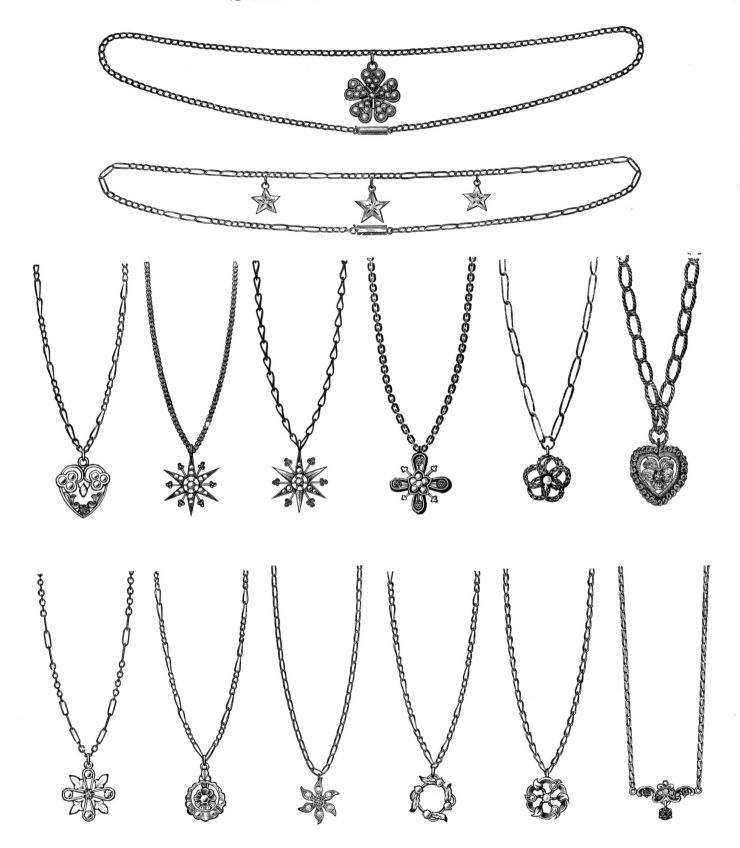

Rolled Gold Plate Necklaces

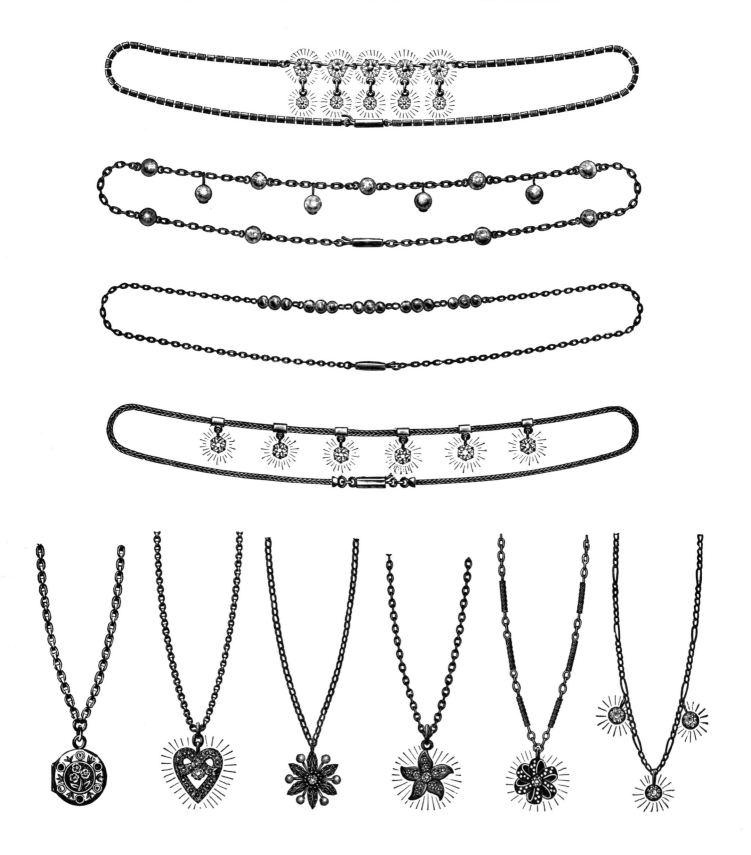

Solid Gold Cuff or Baby Pins

Rolled Gold Plate and Silver Cuff or Baby Pins

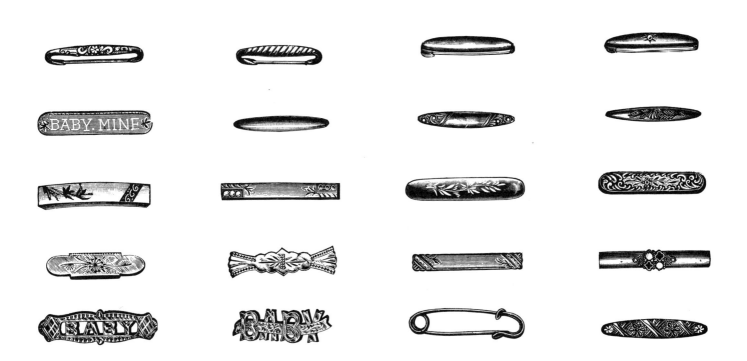

Rolled Gold Plate Pin Sets

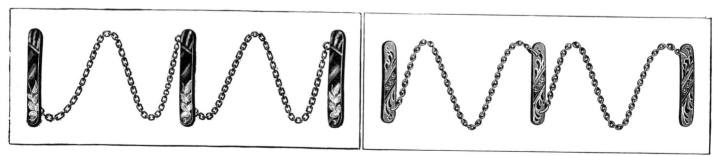

Solid Gold Scarf Pins

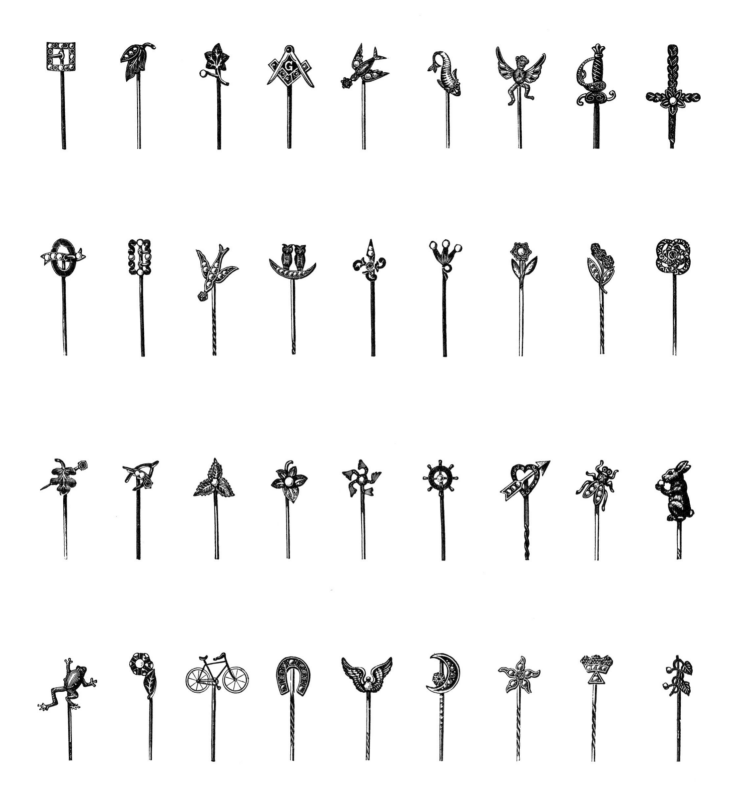

Solid Gold, Silver and Rolled Plate Hat Pins

Rolled Gold Plate Hair Pins.

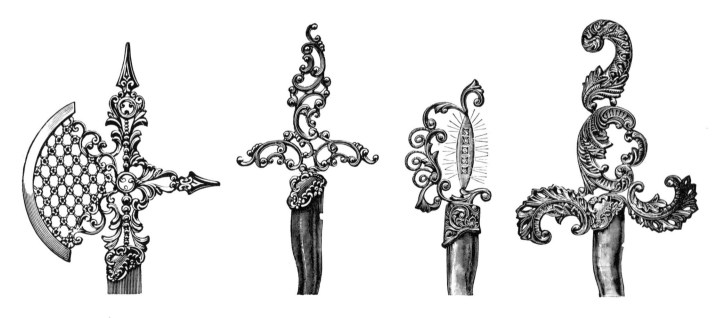

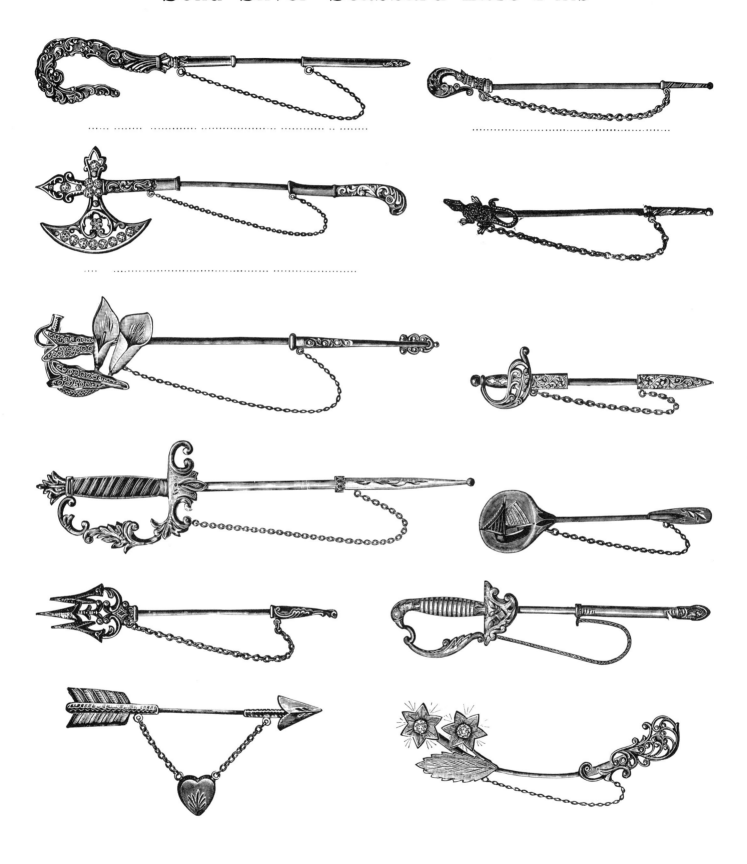

Rolled Gold Plate Scabbard Pins

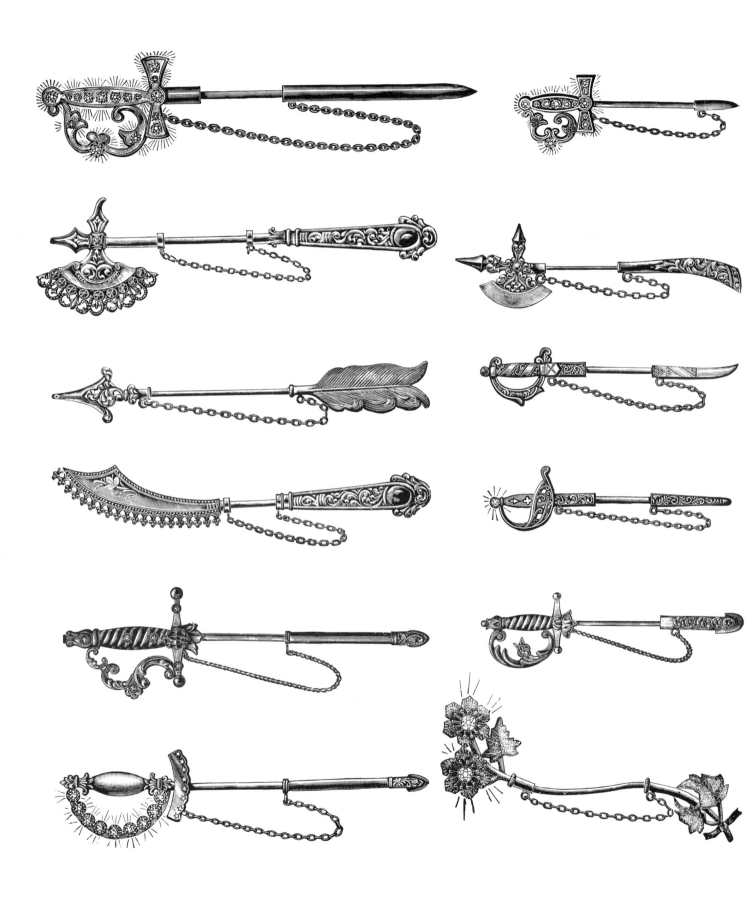

Diamond Jewelry

LACE PINS WITH REMOVABLE SCABBARDS

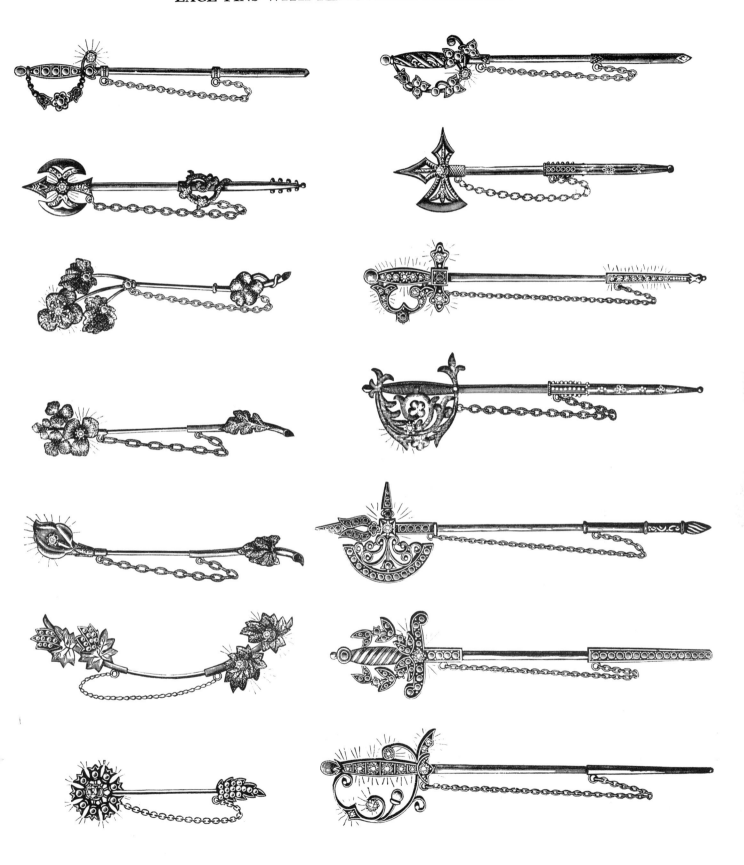

Solid Gold Emblem Charms

KNIGHTS OF PYTHIAS

Enameled.

Enameled.

Enameled.

Enameled.

Enameled.

Enameled.

Enameled,
Raised Bible Back.

Enameled.

Enameled, Bible Back.

Enameled,
Raised Bible Back.

Enameled,
Raised Bible Back.

Enameled,
Raised Bible Back.

Enameled,
Raised Bible Back.

3 Colors of Stone, Diam. in
Sword or Battle Axes.
Raised Bible Back.

Enameled,
Raised Bible Back.

Garnet Eyes.

Enameled,
Skull and Bone, Back.

Enameled,
K. of P. & O. F. Combined.

Enameled.
Skull and Bones Back.

Enameled,
Skull and Bones Back.

Enameled, Back Like 5193.

Enameled, Skull and
Bones Back, Garnet Eyes.

Enameled, Back No. 5201.

Enameled.

Solid Gold Emblem Charms

Knights of Pythias, Enameled.

Knights of Pythias, Onyx Front, Encrusted, Plain Back.

Knights of Pythias, Enameled.

U. R. Knights of Pythias, Enameled.

Knights of Pythias, Bible Back, Enameled.

Knights of Pythias, Colored Onyx, Inlaid, Bible Back.

Knights of Pythias, Enameled.

Knights of Pythias, Enameled.

Knights of Pythias, Enameled.

Knights of Pythias, Enameled.

Knights of Pythias, Skull and Bones Back, Enameled.

Knights of Pythias, Bible Back, Enameled.

Knights of Pythias, Black Enameled Front, Raised Emblem, Plain Back.

Knights of Pythias, Onyx Front, Enameled, Plain Back.

Knights of Pythias, Onyx Base, Enameled.

Knights of Pythias, Enameled.

Knights of Pythias, Bible Back, Enameled.

Knights of Pythias, Bible Back, Enameled.

Knights of Pythias, Enameled, Garnet Eyes, Raised Bible Back.

Knights of Pythias, Enameled Skull and Bones Back, Garnet Eyes.

Knights of Pythias, U. R. Enameled. Back like

Knights of Pythias, Enameled, F. C. B. Back, Center Plain.

Knights of Pythias, Bible Back.

Knights of Pythias, Skull and Bone Back.

Solid Gold Emblem Charms

KNIGHTS TEMPLAR, 32ND DEGREE, ETC.

BACK.   FRONT.

FRONT.   BACK.   BACK.   FRONT.

KNIGHT TEMPLARS

This cut represents back
of all Charms with Locket.

Solid Gold Emblem Charms

MASONIC, ODD FELLOWS, ETC.

| Onyx Front, Raised Emblem, Plain Back. | Enamelled, Plain Back. | Enamelled Emblem Both Sides. | Engraved Both Sides. | Enamelled Both Sides. | Engraved Both Sides. |

Above are Masonic.

Enamelled, Plain Back, Eastern Star.   Enamelled, Plain Back, Eastern Star.   Enameled, Keystone.   **White** Onyx, Gold Frame, Keystone.   Black Enamelled Front, Raised Emblem, Plain Back, Keystone.   Black Enamelled Front, Raised Emblem, Plain Back, Masonic.

Enamelled, Plain Back. Eastern Star.   Engraved. Odd Fellows.   Onyx Front, Raised Emblem, Plain Back.   Enamelled. Odd Fellows.   Enamelled. Odd Fellows.   Black Enamelled Front, Raised Emblem. Plain Back. Odd Fellows.

Enamelled. **Knight of Mystic Chain.**   Enamelled, Garnet Eyes, Raised All-Seeing Eye Back. Odd Fellows.   Enamelled, Raised Bible Back. Odd Fellows.   Enamelled Garnet Eyes, Raised All-Seeing Eye Back. Odd Fellows' Encampment.   Odd Fellows Encampment.   Black Enamelled Front, Raised Emblem, Plain Back. Odd Fellows' Encampment.

Rolled Gold Plate Emblem Charms

233

Odd Fellow, Enamelled
Raised Emblem.

Knights of Pythias,
Enamelled Raised Emblem
Bible on Back in Relief.

Knights of Maccabees,
Enamelled Raised
Emblem.

Benevolent Order of Elks,
Enamelled Raised
Emblem.

Order of Railroad
Conductors, Enamelled
Raised Emblem.

Ancient Order United
Workmen, Raised
Enamelled Emblem.

Masonic,
Chased Raised Emblem.

Odd Fellow,
Chased Raised Emblem.

Odd Fellow
Encampment, Enamelled
Raised Emblem.

Knights of Pythias,
Enamelled Raised
Emblem.

Junior Order American
Mechanics, Enamelled
Raised Emblem.

Knights of the Golden
Eagle, Enamelled Raised
Emblem.

Masonic, Enamelled
Raised Emblem.

Odd Fellows, Chased
Raised Emblem.

Odd Fellows, Enam-
elled Raised Emblem.

Knights of ythias,
Enamelled Raised
Emblem.

Junior Order American
Mechanics, Enamelled
Raised Emblem.

Ancient Order of Forest-
ers, Enamelled Raised
Emblem.

American Railway
Union, Enamelled Raised
Emblem.

Brotherhood Railroad
Trainmen, Enamelled
Raised Emblem.

Benevolent Order of Elks,
Enamelled Raised
Emblem.

American Protective
Association, Enamelled
Raised Emblem.

Red Men, Enamelled
Raised Emblem.

Order Railroad
Conductors, Enamelled
Raised Emblem.

Brotherhood
of Railroad Trainmen,
Enamelled.

Jr. O. Am. Mechanics,
Enamelled Black Onyx,
Front, Polished Back.

Red Men,
Enamelled, Black Onyx
Front, Polished Back.

Knights of Pythias,
Enamelled, Black Onyx
Front, Polished Back.

Masonic,
Enamelled, Black Onyx
Front, Polished Back.

Odd Fellows,
Enamelled, Black Onyx
Front, Polished Back.

234

Rolled Gold Plate Emblem Charms

Jr. Order American Mechanics, Enameled.

Royal Arcanum, Enameled.

Knights of Maccabees, Enameled.

Knights of Pythias, Enameled.

Odd Fellows, Enameled.

Ancient Order United Workmen, Enameled Both Sides.

Knights of Maccabees, Pearl Center, Enameled Emblem Both Sides.

Patriotic Order Sons of America, Pearl Center, Enameled Emblem Both Sides.

Knights of Pythias, Pearl Center, Enameled Emblem Both Sides.

Odd Fellows, Pearl Center, Enameled Emblem Both Sides.

Masonic, Pearl Center, Enameled Emblem Both Sides.

Masonic, Enameled Emblem Both Sides.

Eastern Star, Enameled Front, Plain Back.

Ancient Order United Workmen, Enameled Emblem Both Sides.

Knights of Pythias, Enameled Emblem Both Sides.

Odd Fellows, Enameled Emblem Both Sides.

Masonic, Enameled Emblem Both Sides.

Knights of Pythias, Enameled Both Sides.

Royal Arcanum, Raised Crown, Rubies Inlaid.

Royal Arcanum, Enameled.

Independent Order Foresters, Enameled.

Ancient Order of Foresters, Enameled.

Junior Order American Mechanics, Enameled.

Patriotic Order Sons of America, Enameled.

Masonic, Enameled.

Masonic, Enameled Front, Engraved Back.

Masonic and Odd Fellows Combined, Enameled Front, Engraved Back.

Masonic, Engraved Both Sides.

Masonic and Odd Fellow Combined, Engraved Both Sides.

Masonic and I. O. O. F. Combined, Engraved.

Solid Gold Emblem Charms

Junior Order American Mechanics, Enameled.

Junior Order American Mechanics, Enameled.

Junior Order American Mechanics, Enameled.

Junior Order American Mechanics, Enameled.

Junior Order American Mechanics, Enameled.

Junior Order American Mechanics, Enameled.

FRONT. BACK.
Grand Army of the Republic, Enameled
Same, Plain Back

Eastern Star, Enameled.

Eastern Star, Enameled.

Eastern Star, Enameled.

Eastern Star, Enameled.

Ancient Order United Workmen, Enameled.

Ancient Order United Workmen, Enameled.

Ancient Order United Workmen, Enameled.

Ancient Order United Workmen, Enameled.

Brotherhood of Locomotive Firemen, Enameled.

Brotherhood of Locomotive Engineers, Enameled

Brotherhood of Locomotive Firemen, Enameled.

Brotherhood of Locomotive Engineers, Enameled.

Order of Railroad Conductors, Enameled.

Sons of Veterans, Enameled.

Grand Army, Enameled.

Brotherhood of Railroad Trainmen, Enameled.

Solid Gold Emblem and Plain Charms

Epworth League,

Epworth League,

Epworth League,

Epworth League,

Epworth League,

Epworth League,

Sons of Herman,

Shield of Honor,

Women's Relief Corps,

Daughters of Rebecca,

Daughters of Rebecca,

Daughters of Rebecca,

Knights of Columbus,

Knight of Columbus,

League American Wheel-
men, Enameled.

Red Men, Enameled.

Knights of St. John,
Enameled.

Knights of Malta,
Enameled.

Knights of Macabees,

Ladies of Macabees,

Knights of Macabees,

Solid Gold Emblem Pins
VARIOUS ORDERS

Brotherhood of **Railway Trainmen,** Engraved. — Order Railway Conductors, Enamelled. — Brotherhood of Railway Conductors. Enamelled. — Order Railway Conductors, Enamelled.

ALL THE ABOVE ARE BROTHERHOOD OF LOCOMOTIVE ENGINEERS AND FIREMEN.

Order Railway Conductors, Enamelled. — Order Railway Conductors, Engraved. — Order Railway Conductors, Enamelled. — Order Railway Conductors, Engraved. — Order Railway Conductors, Enamelled. — Brotherhood of Railway Trainmen, Enamelled. — Brotherhood of Railway Trainmen, Enamelled. — Brotherhood of Railway Trainmen, Enamelled.

Brotherhood of Railway Trainmen, Enamelled. — Brotherhood of Railway Trainmen, Enamelled. — Brotherhood of Railway Trainmen, Enamelled. — Brotherhood of Railway Trainmen, Enamelled. — Brotherhood of Railway Trainmen, Enamelled. — Brotherhood of Railway Trainmen, Enamelled. — Switchmen, Enamelled. — Switchmen, Enamelled.

Order of Railway **Telegraph.** Enam'd. — Order of Railway Telegraph. Enam'd. — American Railway Union, Enamelled. — American Railway Union, Enamelled. — American Railway Union, Enamelled. — Engineer, Enamelled. — Conductor. Enamelled.

Solid Gold Emblem Pins

MASONIC

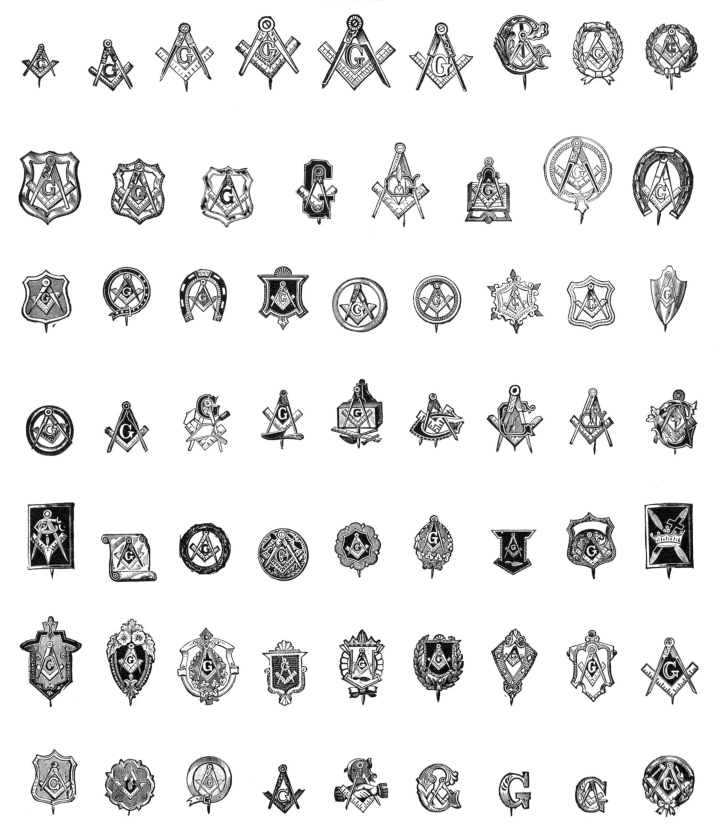

Rolled Gold Plate Emblem Lapel Buttons and Pins

VARIOUS ORDERS

Mystic Shrine, Enameled. | Mystic Shrine, Enameled. | Mystic Shrine, Ruby Inlaid, Enameled. | Mystic Shrine, Enameled. | Mystic Shrine, Enameled. | Masonic and I. O. O. F., Enameled. | Masonic, Enameled. | Knight Templar, Enameled. | Keystone, Enameled.

Odd Fellows Encampment, Enameled. | Odd Fellows, Enameled. | Knight of Pythias, Enameled. | P. O. S. of America, Enameled. | Knights of the Golden Eagle, Enameled. | American Legion of Honor, Enameled. | Epworth League, Enameled. | Royal Arcanum, Enameled. | Young Men's Christian Ass'n, Enameled.

I. O. of Foresters, Raised Head, Enameled. | I. O. of Foresters, Enameled. | I. O. of Foresters, Enameled. | I.O.of Foresters, Enameled. | B. P. O. of Elks, Enameled. | B. P. O. of Elks, Raised Head, Enameled. | Knights of Malta, Enameled. | Modern Woodman of America, Enameled. | League of American Wheelmen, Enameled.

Heptasoph, Enameled. | Knights of Columbus, Enameled. | B. R. R. Trainmen, Enameled. | Brotherhood of Locomotive Firemen, Enameled. | Brotherhood Locomotive Engineers, Enameled. | Senior Order Am. Mechanics, Enameled. | Ancient Order United Workmen Enameled. | Ancient Order United Workmen Enameled. | Independent Order Mechanics, Enameled.

Knights of Honor Enameled. | Ancient Order Hibernians, Enameled. | Knights of the Ancient Essenic, Enameled. | National Union, Enameled. | Orient of Junior Mechanics, Enameled. | Sons of Veterans, Enameled. | Grand Army. Enameled. | Catholic Mutual Benevolent Ass'n Enameled. | Catholic T. A. Union of Am., Enameled.

Red Men, Enameled. | Red Men, Enameled. | Catholic Order of Foresters, Enameled. | Fraternal Mystic Circle, Enameled. | Grand Orient, Enameled. | Royal League, Enameled. | Daughters of America, Enameled. | Mystic Charm, Enameled.

Masonic, Enameled. | Masonic, Enameled. | Masonic, Engraved. | Masonic, Enameled. | Odd Fellows, Chased. | Odd Fellows, Chased. | Odd Fellows, Chased. | Odd Fellows, Enameled.

Odd Fellows, Enameled. | Odd Fellows, Enameled. | Odd Fellows, Chased. | Catholic Mutual Benevolent Ass'n Enameled. | Young Men's Christian Ass'n, Enameled. | League of Am. Wheelmen, Enameled, Garnet Center. | Catholic Order of Foresters, Enameled. | Ladies' Catholic Benevolent Ass'n Enameled.

VARIOUS ORDERS

Eastern Star, Enameled.

Eastern Star, Enameled.

Eastern Star, Enameled.

Junior Order American Mechanics, Enameled.

Junior Order, American Mechanics, Enameled.

Junior Order American Mechanics Enameled.

Odd Fellows, Enameled.

Odd Fellows Encampment, Enameled.

Knights of Pythias, Enameled.

Knights of Pythias, Enameled.

Knights of Pythias, Enameled.

Knights of Pythias, Enameled.

Royal Neighbors, Enameled.

Knights of the Golden Eagle. Enameled.

Junior Order United Am. Mechanics, Enameled.

Modern Woodmen of America, Enameled.

Ancient Order of Foresters, Enameled.

Independent Order of Foresters, Enameled.

Ancient Order United Workmen,

Ancient Order United Workmen,

Knights of the Maccabees,

Knights of the Maccabees,

Knights of the Maccabees,

Knights of the Maccabees,

Daughters of America, Enameled.

Daughters of Rebecca, Enameled.

Daughters of Rebecca, Enameled.

Royal Arcanum, Enameled.

Knights of the World, Enameled.

Mystic Chain, Enameled.

Epworth League. Enameled

Epworth League. Enameled.

Knights of Honor, Enameled.

Knights of Honor, Enameled.

Catholic Mutual Benevolent Ass'n, Enameled.

Sons of Herman, Enameled.

Redmen, Enameled.

Redmen, Enameled.

Redmen, Enameled.

Redmen, Enameled.

Ladies of the Maccabees, Enameled.

Ladies of the Maccabees, Enameled.

Catholic T. A. U. of Am., Enameled.

Good Templars, Enameled.

Woodman of the World, Enameled.

Brotherhood of Ry. Trainmen. Enam.

Grand Army, Enameled.

Sons of Veterans, Enameled.

Daughters of Rebecca, Enameled.

Daughters of Liberty, Enameled.

Royal Arcanum, Enameled.

Woman's Relief Corps, Enameled.

Independent Order of Foresters.

Eastern Star, Enameled.

Eastern Star, Enameled.

Ladies Knights of Honor, Enameled,

242

Solid Gold Emblem Pins

Epworth League.

Epworth League,

Epworth League,

Epworth League,

Epworth League,

Ladies of
The Macabees,

Ladies of
The Macabees,

P. O. Sons of
America,

Daughter of
Rebecca,
Enamelled.

ood Templars,
Enamelled.

Junior Order
American
Mechanics.

Ladies of
The Macabees,
Enamelled.

Ladies of
The Macabees,
Enamelled.

Modern Woodman
of America,
Enamelled.

Knights of Pythias,
Enamelled.

Brotherhood
Locomotive Fire-
men.

Eastern Star,

Eastern Star,

Eastern Star,

Daughter of
Rebecca,

Eastern Star,

Eastern Star,

Eastern Star,

Eastern Star,

Junior Order United
American Mechanics,

American
Railway Union,

International Asso-
ciation of Machinists,

Woman's
Relief Corps,

Pythian Sisterhood,

Independent
Order Foresters,

Eastern Star,

Companion of
Forest.

Eastern Star,

Eastern Star,

Knights of the
Golden Eagle,

Knights and Ladies
of Honor,

B. P. O. Elks,

B. P. O. Elks,

Knights and
Ladies of Honor,

Ancient Order
United Workmen,